Returning from the Abyss

Pivotal Moments in the Old Testament

Brent A. Strawn, *Series Editor*

Other books in this series:

Delivered out of Empire: Pivotal Moments in the Book of Exodus, Part One

Delivered into Covenant: Pivotal Moments in the Book of Exodus, Part Two

Returning from the Abyss

Pivotal Moments in the Book of Jeremiah

Walter Brueggemann

WESTMINSTER
JOHN KNOX PRESS
LOUISVILLE · KENTUCKY

First edition
Published by Westminster John Knox Press
Louisville, Kentucky

22 23 24 25 26 27 28 29 30 31—10 9 8 7 6 5 4 3 2 1

Book design by Sharon Adams
Cover design by Nita Ybarra and Allison Taylor
Cover illustration: At Every Mass We Reach Up and Meet the Father through the Sacrifice of Christ Our Head, Bound Together with Each Other and with Him, *2002 (oil on board), Wang, Elizabeth (1942–2016) / © Radiant Light / Bridgeman Images*

Library of Congress Cataloging-in-Publication Data

Names: Brueggemann, Walter, author.
Title: Returning from the abyss : pivotal moments in the Book of Jeremiah / Walter Brueggemann.
Description: First edition. | Louisville, Kentucky : Westminster John Knox Press, [2022] | Includes bibliographical references. | Summary: "Explores the historical and literary context of the book of Jeremiah, drawing out pivotal moments in the text to illuminate the dual themes of Israel's long walk into, and out of, the trauma and devastation of exile"-- Provided by publisher.
Identifiers: LCCN 2021060162 (print) | LCCN 2021060163 (ebook) | ISBN 9780664266868 (paperback) | ISBN 9781646982462 (ebook)
Subjects: LCSH: Bible. Jeremiah--Criticism, interpretation, etc.
Classification: LCC BS1525.52 .B787 2022 (print) | LCC BS1525.52 (ebook) | DDC 224/.206--dc23/eng/20220127
LC record available at https://lccn.loc.gov/2021060162
LC ebook record available at https://lccn.loc.gov/2021060163

Most Westminster John Knox Press books are available at special quantity discounts when purchased in bulk by corporations, organizations, and special-interest groups. For more information, please e-mail SpecialSales@wjkbooks.com.

For
Jim Wallis

Contents

viii   Contents

Series Foreword

Pivots in Scripture

*N*ot long after arriving in Atlanta for my first tenure-track job, still very green in my field and profession, I somehow found the courage to invite Walter Brueggemann, who taught a few miles away at Columbia Theological Seminary, to lecture in my Introduction to Old Testament course. To my great delight he accepted, despite the fact that the class met at eight o'clock in the morning and Atlanta traffic is legendary. (Those who know Walter better than I did at that time know what I discovered only later: that such generosity is standard operating procedure for him.) I either offered, or perhaps he suggested, that the topic of his guest lecture should be Jeremiah. And so it was that a few weeks after the invitation was extended and received, my students and I were treated to eighty minutes of brilliant insight into Jeremiah from one of the masters of that biblical book, not to mention the larger Book to which Jeremiah belongs.[1]

Even now, twenty years later, I remember a number of things about that lecture—clear testimony to the quality of the content and the one who gave it. In all honesty, I must admit that several of the things I remember have made their way into my own subsequent lectures on Jeremiah. In this way, Walter's presence could still (and *still can*) be felt in my later classes, despite the fact that I couldn't ask him to guest lecture every year (alas!). One moment from that initial lecture stands out with special clarity: Walter's exposition of a specific text from Jeremiah 30. I suspect I knew this particular text before, maybe even read about it in something Walter had written, but as I recall things now it was that early morning lecture at Emory

ix

University in 2002 that drilled it into my long-term memory banks. The text in question was Jeremiah 30:12–17:[2]

¹²For thus says the LORD:
Your hurt is incurable,
   your wound is grievous.
¹³There is no one to uphold your cause,
   no medicine for your wound,
   no healing for you.
¹⁴All your lovers have forgotten you;
   they care nothing for you;
for I have dealt you the blow of an enemy,
   the punishment of a merciless foe,
because your guilt is great,
   because your sins are so numerous.
¹⁵Why do you cry out over your hurt?
   Your pain is incurable.
Because your guilt is great,
   because your sins are so numerous,
   I have done these things to you.
¹⁶Therefore all who devour you shall be devoured,
   and all your foes, every one of them, shall go into captivity;
those who plunder you shall be plundered,
   and all who prey on you I will make a prey.
¹⁷For I will restore health to you,
   and your wounds I will heal,

                     says the LORD,

because they have called you an outcast:
   "It is Zion; no one cares for her!"

The passage is striking for a number of reasons, but what Walter highlighted was the remarkable shift—or better, *pivot*—that takes place in the space between verses 15 and 16. Prior to this point, God's speech to Israel emphasizes the incurable nature of its wound: "no healing for you" (v. 13)! Israel's wound is, on the one hand,

   the blow of an *enemy*,
   the punishment of a *merciless foe* (v. 14).

On the other hand, the blow is also and more fundamentally *God's own doing*:

for *I have dealt* you the blow (v. 14)
I have done these things to you (v. 15).

Like the original audience, contemporary readers are left no time to ponder this double-agency since immediately after the second ascription of this wound to the Lord's hand, the text pivots both suddenly and drastically. From verse 16 on, we read that those whom the Lord used to punish Israel will now themselves be punished; we also learn that what had before been a terminal illness turns out to be treatable after all (v. 17a). The reason for this dramatic shift is given only in verse 17b: God will cure the incurable wound because God will not stand by while Israel's enemies call it "an outcast," claiming that "no one cares for Zion."

Now in truth, what God says to Israel/Zion in verse 13 sounds very much like "no one cares for you," but as Walter memorably put it in his lecture, while it is one thing to talk about your own mother, it is another thing altogether when *someone else* talks about your mother! God, it would seem, claims privilege to say certain things about Zion that others are simply not allowed to say. If and when they ever do utter such sentiments, God is mobilized to defend and to heal. Zion, it turns out, is no outcast, after all; there is, after all, at least One who still cares for her.

The space between verses 15 and 16 is a *pivot*, explained most fully in verse 17. This, then, is a turning point that changes everything in this passage—a passage that can be seen, more broadly and in turn, as a pivotal moment in the larger book of Jeremiah, coming, as it does, early in a section that shifts decidedly toward consolation and restoration.

And Jeremiah 30:12–17 is not alone in the Old Testament. Another remarkable pivot takes place in the space between the two lines of Psalm 22:21:

Save me from the mouth of the lion!
From the horns of the wild oxen you have rescued me.

In the first line, there is an urgent plea for immediate help: "Save!"; in the second, testimony to past deliverance: "You *have rescued* me." Something drastic, something pivotal has taken place here, in between two parallel lines of Hebrew poetry. Before this pivot, the psalmist knew only of *God-forsakenness* (v. 1). But after it, the psalmist is full only of *God-praise* (vv. 22–24) that extends to the most remarkable and unexpected corners of the world and underworld (vv. 25–31).[3]

Spiritual writer and humanities professor Marilyn Chandler McEntyre has written recently of "pausing where Scripture gives one pause."[4] She comments on memorable biblical phrases like "teach me your paths," "hidden with Christ," and "do not harden your hearts." Phrases like these, she writes,

> have lives of their own. Neither sentences nor single words, they are little compositions that suggest and evoke and invite. . . . They are often what we remember: "Fourscore and seven years ago" recalls a whole era, triggers a constellation of feelings, and evokes an image of Lincoln. . . . In the classic film *A Bridge Too Far*, one soldier, rowing for his life away from an impending explosion, repeats again and again a fragment of the only prayer he remembers: "Hail Mary, full of grace . . . Hail Mary, full of grace . . . Hail Mary, full of grace . . ."—and somehow we believe that such a prayer at such a time suffices.[5]

So it is that key phrases are "powerful instruments of awakening and recollection for all of us."[6] McEntyre goes on to note that the spiritual practice of meditative reading known as *lectio divina* encourages readers to pay attention to specific words or phrases:

> Learning to notice what we notice as we move slowly from words to meaning, pausing where we sense a slight beckoning, allowing associations to emerge around the phrase that stopped us is an act of faith that the Spirit will meet us there. There is, we may assume, a gift to be received wherever we are stopped and summoned.[7]

Pivotal moments in the Old Testament like the ones in Jeremiah 30 and Psalm 22 aren't exactly the same thing as the practice of pausing commended by McEntyre, but the two seem closely related nevertheless. Pivotal texts are precisely the ones that arrest us, demand our attention, change everything:

* Suddenly, *healing*—Jeremiah 30:16–17
* Suddenly, *deliverance*—Psalm 22:21b

Of course, the pivots found in Scripture are not always so benign. One may think, alternatively, of these:

- Suddenly, *trouble*—as in 2 Samuel 11:5, Bathsheba's report (only two words in Hebrew) to David: "I'm pregnant."
- Suddenly, *judgment*—as in 2 Samuel 12:7, Nathan's statement (also only two words in Hebrew) to David: "You're that man!"

Now one could, especially in a more skeptical mode, wonder just how many pivotal moments, how many *suddenlys* like these, might actually exist in Scripture. But before we assume that the list is quite finite—more of a curiosity than a persistent call to attention—and take our leave to attend to some piece of distracting drivel on our electronic devices, we should stop and remember the Gospel of Mark, which makes a living on *suddenlys*. Jesus is always doing something or having something done to him *suddenly* or *immediately* (*euthus*), and the same is often true for those gathered around him.[8]

What Mark shows us is that, in the end, *suddenly* can aptly describe an entire Gospel, an entire life lived toward God—indeed, a life lived most perfectly toward God. The same may be true for the gospel of God writ large, across both testaments of the Christian Bible. And so, along with the practice of pausing where Scripture gives us pause (McEntyre), the practice of pivoting where Scripture itself pivots has the same effect: it turns us toward something new, something deeper, something *transformative*. These texts are places where the Bible, and we who read it, may pivot toward another world—another *divine* world—that can change our own world for the better, forever. In contrast to McEntyre's pauses, which anticipate that the Spirit will reach out to us through the text, these pivotal moments in Scripture are not acts of faith but *places* of faith, established sites where the Spirit has *already* met the faithful. They are gifts *already* given, though they seem largely still waiting on us to receive them. The goal of the present volume, and this series dedicated to pivotal moments in the Old Testament, is to mediate those gifts. We are fortunate to have Professor Brueggemann lead the way.

Brent A. Strawn, *Series Editor*

Preface

*T*his book is an invitation to a sustained study of the book of Jeremiah. This invitation is issued to pastors, church members, and other serious readers. As with other books in this series, this book is organized in brief expositions of specific verses of the book of Jeremiah. It is my intention that each such exposition might be readily accessible for reading and reflection without undue attention to too much background. It is, moreover, my expectation that if these verses are taken in sequence, by the end of the study the reader will have a good sense of Jeremiah even though this prophetic book is quite complex. I have sought to introduce the *literary and historical complexity* of the book of Jeremiah, all the while keeping one eye on the *primary plotline* of the book.

That plotline pivots around the abyss experienced in the destruction of Jerusalem in 587 BCE and the resultant deportation of leading inhabitants of the city into exile in Babylon. The work of the prophet, first, is to break the illusion of the city and its leadership in the run-up to the destruction by an assertion that a political economy organized against the will of the God of covenant cannot prevail. Conversely, once the destruction has occurred, it is the prophetic task to foster hope for restoration and return. Thus Jeremiah's work is to *walk Israel into the abyss of exile* (in the face of denial) and then to *walk Israel out of that abyss* (in the face of despair).

It has long been my pedagogical mantra concerning the book of Jeremiah that "it reads like it was written yesterday." That is, the book teems with stunning contemporaneity. "Contemporaneity" in Scripture study is a quite tricky matter, because it evokes all kinds of poor analogues and highly subjective "applications" to our time and place. My use of "contemporaneity" intends something other than that. Rather, I mean to suggest that the plotline of the book of Jeremiah—*into abyss / out of abyss*—is a plotline to which sober American Christians can pay attention. The "Christian" part of that contemporaneity is that the *into abyss / out of abyss* plot, in the Jesus narrative, morphs into *Friday crucifixion* and *Sunday resurrection*. Beyond that specificity in the Jesus narrative, moreover, I want to suggest that the plotline of ancient Israel can illuminate the plotline of U.S. history. First, Israel was, so the prophet contends, walking toward self-destruction for a very long time, even though in its "chosenness" Israel did not notice that slippery slope toward destruction. Thus it was easy in a self-satisfied Jerusalem to say "peace, peace" when there was no peace (Jeremiah 6:14; 8:11). The United States, the more it has moved to become an empire and world power and the more it has depended on the cheap labor of slavery with concomitant self-indulgence, the more it has contradicted the will of the creator God. In our prosperity, however, we mostly have not noticed the slip toward self-destruction. In ancient Israel that long, slow slope culminated in the inescapable wake-up call of 587 BCE at the hands of the Babylonians. In like manner, I suggest, the crisis of 9/11 constituted a brusque wake-up call summoning us away from the smug confidence in exceptionalism, asserting that "chosenness" for the United States was no guarantee against the untamed work of the historical process through which the inscrutable holiness of God is at work. Since 2001, the news and various circumstances—especially the multiple pandemics experienced in COVID-19, racial injustice, and socioeconomic disparity—have only served to uncover the lies that lie at the root of "the American Dream."

Second, as it faced loss, destruction, and displacement, Israel easily enough could slide into despair about its future (see, for example, Ezekiel 37:11). In that circumstance, it was the task of the prophet to articulate new historical possibility, albeit in poetic anticipation. In like manner, given the obvious failure of the social fabric of the United States and the inability of our political economy to keep its promises to the "left behind," it is easy enough among us to despair of any viable future for the United States that would convincingly embody "the American Dream." In such circumstance,

the prophetic task is to foster hope that might be costly and incon-
venient but that might provide energy, courage, and imagination
for a just and moral economic-political historical future. It was
exactly the rhetoric of Martin Luther King in his "dream speech"
that invited us to such a restorative vision and to the risky work that
such a vision would entail.

It is my hope that as readers invest in this study of Jeremiah, they
will be able more knowingly to situate themselves in *the plotline
of destruction and restoration* as voiced in the book of Jeremiah as
it pertains to the United States, with our long-standing racism and
economic injustice. Without "applying" the text of Jeremiah to our
circumstance with any specificity, it is possible and useful to allow
this ancient text to seed our imagination in fresh discernment concerning both our past and present historical realities and our future
historical possibilities. Such reseeded imagination works from the
assumption that the creator God who makes covenant has a will and
intention distinct from the world (and from us!) that cannot be easily
or safely disregarded. The gods of the establishment who occupy the
dominant narrative are, in contrast to the Lord of the covenant, quite
benign and irrelevant. Thus Jeremiah can see that his own people
worshiped gods who

> cannot do evil,
> nor is it in them to do good.
> 10:5

Likewise mighty Babylon, cipher for every imperial power, wor-
ships gods of whom the poet says,

> There is no breath in them.
> They are worthless, a work of delusion.
> 51:17–18

So it is with the gods of white capitalist nationalism. These are
the gods of "our thoughts and prayers that are with the victims" who
never make any difference for the victims. The book of Jeremiah, in
all of its complexity, attests a very different theological reality that
impinges in real ways upon historical processes. Any serious reader
of Jeremiah may consider how this claim concerning the intentionality of a holy God matters, and how that claim impels the way we

understand the plotline of our historical experience. We, too, face the abyss and are walking resolutely into it. Jeremiah helps us see that. Jeremiah also offers a way to return, come back, even repent from that abyss.

This book is not a full-scale commentary on the book of Jeremiah. I have written such a commentary,[1] and I am also indebted to a host of other Jeremiah interpreters, most especially my friends Kathleen O'Connor, Carolyn Sharp, and Louis Stulman, but also John Bracke, Ronald Clements, Terry Fretheim, and Patrick Miller. Readers who want to go further into the book of Jeremiah can readily consult their felicitous studies.

I am glad to dedicate this book with great appreciation to Jim Wallis. There is no one in the recent generation among us who has so compellingly and faithfully practiced prophetic ministry as Jim. He has constantly told the hard truth about our society. He has, beyond that hard truth, articulated faithful ways forward toward a neighborly society, not least in his recent initiative concerning "Reclaiming Jesus." As the founder and point person for the Sojourners community, he is not unlike the scribal community attached to Jeremiah led by the two sons of Neriah, Baruch and Seriah (see Jeremiah 36:4 and 51:59, respectively). The work of such a community is to keep alive the testimony of faith; Jim's work with the Sojourners community has done just that. My debts to him are great and abiding.

Walter Brueggemann

Suggested Sessions for Study Groups

Week 1	=	Chapters 1–2
Week 2	=	Chapters 3–5
Week 3	=	Chapters 6–7
Week 4	=	Chapters 8–10
Week 5	=	Chapters 11–12
Week 6	=	Chapters 13–14
Week 7	=	Chapters 15–16
Week 8	=	Chapters 17–18
Week 9	=	Chapters 19–21
Week 10	=	Chapters 22–23
Week 11	=	Chapters 24–25
Week 12	=	Chapters 26–27

Chapter 1

The Word of the Lord "Came" (and Still Does) (Jeremiah 1:3)

It came also in the days of King Jehoiakim son of Josiah of Judah, and until the end of the eleventh year of King Zedekiah son of Josiah of Judah, until the captivity of Jerusalem in the fifth month.

Scripture Passages for Reference

Jeremiah 1:1–3
2 Samuel 8:13
1 Kings 1:13, 25
2 Kings 22–23

The book of Jeremiah opens with an editorial introduction (1:1–3). These verses are likely a notation added later by scribes; they give us important data that serve as clues about how to read the book that follows. The "it" of verse 3 is "the word of the LORD" that was uttered and enacted through the long historical period that concerns the book. We are not told how the word of the Lord "came." Verse 2 tells us that it came to Jeremiah the prophet; thereafter the prophet uttered his own words that became the book. But we are also permitted to think that "the word of the LORD," as the exercise of divine sovereignty, "came" in and through the historical processes that are reflected in the book of Jeremiah. Either way, or in both ways, what follows is testimony about the way in which the sovereign will of YHWH impinged upon the historical processes of Jerusalem. It is to this impingement, by utterance and by action, that the words of Jeremiah and the words of his book bear witness. What follows in the book is a consideration of the odd interface between that effective but elusive word of the Lord and the palpable realities of public history.

In order to articulate a timeline and a historical frame of reference for the book of Jeremiah, this editorial introduction mentions three kings in Jerusalem. The first is King Josiah (639–609 BCE), who is elsewhere scarcely present in the book, but his fingerprints are all over it. In 2 Kings 22–23 we are told that King Josiah instituted a great reform in Jerusalem that called Israel back to the realities of the Sinai covenant, realities that had long been disregarded by royal Jerusalem. The reform of Josiah was grounded in the conviction that adherence to the commandments of YHWH was the inescapable precondition of public well-being. It is likely that the "covenant" to which Jeremiah bears witness in Jeremiah 11:6–7 refers to the work of Josiah. The prophet, moreover, reports that "listeners" did not "listen" but promptly and completely rejected the requirements of covenant: "Yet they did not obey or incline their ear." Josiah is referenced, moreover, in Jeremiah 22:15–16 as "your father" (father of Shallum), who did justice for the poor and needy.

The introduction also names Jehoiakim (also called Shallum [609–598]), who is reckoned by Jeremiah to be an evil king who violated covenant by refusing to pay his workers (22:13), thus bringing trouble upon his people. The third king mentioned is Zedekiah (598–587), brother of Jehoiakim, who is portrayed in the book as a vacillating coward who wanted to obey the covenant but who also wanted to appease Babylon (Jeremiah 37–38) and who finally ended as a brutalized failure (52:10). While absent from this introduction, there is a fourth king to be noted, Jehoiachin (598), son of Jehoiakim, also called Coniah. In 22:28–30 he is imagined as a broken potsherd to be cast off—that is, deported to Babylon (more on this later). It is anticipated in the poetry of 22:30 that Jehoiachin will be childless—that is, without an heir. The long-running dynasty of David will come to an end!

Thus the book of Jeremiah has as its context and historical material the sweep of the Davidic dynasty that reaches its apex of faithfulness in Josiah and soon after its nadir of humiliation in the two deported kings, Jehoiachin and Zedekiah. The book of Jeremiah intends to point to the effective operation of the word of the Lord in, with, and under historical vagaries of the Jerusalem sacral-political establishment.

Over against that establishment is set only the single person of Jeremiah. The opening verses want us to see that this adjudication of the rule and interpretation of history is a quite unequal contest. On the one side is the monarchy, with its deep dynastic promises from God. On the other side is only Jeremiah—except we know more of him. We are told in 1:1 that he derives from "the priests of Anathoth," a village in the tribal area of Benjamin not far from Jerusalem. When we scroll back on "the priests of Anathoth" in the Bible, we come to the ancient priest Abiathar, who was one of the two priests of David (2 Samuel 8:18). He was clearly closely connected to royal power (2 Samuel 15:13; 17:3; 19:11).

In the struggle for the succession to the throne after David, however, Abiathar sided with David's son Adonijah (1 Kings 1:19, 25) against the ambitious claim of his other son Solomon. In the end, of course, Solomon prevailed, and the adherents to Adonijah (the loser) were in the disfavor of the new king. Abiathar, the priest, was on the wrong side and was banished by King Solomon to his home village of Anathoth (1 Kings 2:26–27). It is from the rootage of this banished priest that Jeremiah comes. It is credible to think that Abiathar long ago opposed Solomon for king because he anticipated the self-aggrandizement that would mark Solomon's reign. Thus it is credible to think that Jeremiah was heir to this old and deep resistance to Solomon and all that he came to represent in the royal Jerusalem power structure. Jeremiah may be seen as a carrier of long-term critical resentment against the lavish covenant-violating Jerusalem dynasty.

This innocent-looking introduction thus sets up for us the mighty struggle for the truth of history that is to be waged in the book of Jeremiah. This struggle is between the *long-legitimated royal dynasty* and an old *deep critical resentment* that is grounded in the covenantal tradition and the ancient theological conviction that had not been erased by the force of money and power. The reader of the book of Jeremiah is recruited to participate in that struggle for the truth of history. It is an ancient struggle in the purview of biblical faith. The reason we continue to read the book of Jeremiah, however, is that this ancient struggle for the truth of history is at the same time an astonishingly contemporary struggle. And we readers are summoned into that contemporary struggle.

The book of Jeremiah was composed over a long time—as long as all of these kings and beyond. From the outset, however, the makers of the book of Jeremiah and presumably the prophet himself understood the sure outcome of that struggle. They understood the outcome ahead of time because they never doubted that the rule of God, enacted by the word of God, would prevail over the policies of monarchy and temple. They saw, as Jeremiah did, that the monarchy and the royal city were quite temporary affairs in the long story of Israel:

> Our little systems have their day;
> They have their day and cease to be:
> They are but broken lights of thee,
> And thou, O Lord, art more than they.[1]

When we reach the final phrase of our verse, we come to the theme of the book of Jeremiah: "*until the captivity of Jerusalem.*" From the outset, the book and its framers (and the prophet Jeremiah) knew that the entire collection of the book was headed toward and would pivot around the deportation and displacement of the leading members of the Jerusalem regime—the deep abyss of exile. They knew there would be a final king, the last on the royal timeline. They knew the coming end of the dynasty. They knew of the coming destruction of the temple. They knew that the power status of Jerusalem and its dominant narrative could not be sustained, because they contradicted the will and purpose of the Lord of history. In Jeremiah 52:28–30 we are given a sober report concerning the deportations—three times: 598, 587, and 581. Of these, the second is reckoned as the decisive displacement, the ultimate abyss, as it were. In our reading we are struck now by how few were the number of deportees: 4,600. But the impact and durable significance of the deportation, for the book of Jeremiah and for the ongoing faith of Judaism, are quite disproportionate to the actual historical data. The displacement is the defining fracture in the history of God and Israel as God's people. It is a fracture that signifies God's full estrangement from God's people. The deportation is a manifestation of the truth that the will and purpose of YHWH are not tied to any historical reality. YHWH will govern in freedom according to YHWH's own purpose.

It is the work of the book of Jeremiah to reflect on that decisively broken connection. The book is a witness to that reality, but it is also a pastoral enterprise to walk the faithful into the abyss and to dwell there. And then, before the book is finished (and long after the prophet), the work of the book is to walk the faithful back out of the abyss of exile into a new life of fidelity with God. The introduction speaks only "until the captivity." The book itself, however, goes beyond that. It knows that even after the deep fracture there is more, because God is relentlessly passionate for this people and its city that have been so wayward. The book of Jeremiah, from its initial "until," invites its readers into the deep, powerful trauma of *loss to death*, then *new life through inexplicable gift. Into* and *back from* the abyss!

Questions for Discussion

1. How has the Lord's word come in the past? Where do you see it now?

2. Can you imagine a decisive break now like that of the exile for ancient Israel?

3. Do you agree that devastating experiences like the deportations of Judah can be "the will and purpose of God"? How do these experiences show that God's work and will "are not tied to any historical purpose"?

4. What do you think it means or looks like for the Lord to "govern in freedom according to God's own purpose"?

Chapter 2

To Pluck Up . . . and to Plant
(Jeremiah 1:10)

"See, today I appoint you over nations and over kingdoms,
to pluck up and to pull down,
to destroy and to overthrow,
to build and to plant."

Scripture Passages for Reference

Jeremiah 1:4–10
Jeremiah 11:20
Jeremiah 18:7–10
Jeremiah 20:10
Jeremiah 24:7
Jeremiah 31:18
Jeremiah 45:4
Jeremiah 51:64
John 2:19–22
Romans 4:17
1 Corinthians 1:28

Immediately after the editorial introduction of 1:1–3, the book of Jeremiah gets to work in 1:4–10 with a report concerning the divine authorization of Jeremiah as a prophet who will speak the word of the Lord to the people of the Lord. The tricky wording of the introduction

7

makes it clear that the book that follows is not itself the word of the Lord; rather, the book consists of "the words of Jeremiah," who received the word of the Lord. Verses 4–10 tell us why and how Jeremiah is authorized and credentialed as a recipient of the word of the Lord and why his own words are to be trusted and heeded.

Jeremiah 1:4–10 is highly stylized; these verses follow a recurring pattern of speech for the "call" of a prophet. Because of such a stylized way of expression, it is possible that the verbal exchange between Jeremiah and YHWH at the initiative of YHWH in these verses is not an actual report. The text may instead reflect a liturgical convention of how such an uncommon experience was codified and formally enacted in the community. Or it is even possible that the "call narrative" is a literary construction by the editors of the book of Jeremiah to present the figure of Jeremiah in the text as a credible voice for YHWH. Whatever the case, we can see how difficult and how important it was for the book of Jeremiah to find a way to connect *the human speaker Jeremiah* to *the elusive, transcendent, and sovereign YHWH;* a claim of authority for the book of Jeremiah depends on that connection. This particular text serves to make that connection.

When we take this text on its own terms, two things are clear. First, the person of Jeremiah was vigorously resistant to designation as speaker for YHWH. His resistance is expressed as he disclaims any capacity to function as such a speaker: He is too young. He is incompetent for such speech. We see in the later book of Jeremiah that he had good reason to refuse the prophetic task, because the words he had to speak were not welcome and evoked great hostility. The words that he had to speak interrupted the "bubble" of security and self-sufficiency that dominated official Jerusalem. Thus men from his home village threatened him (11:20), and his close friends dismissed him (20:10).

The counterpoint in the "call narrative," however, is equally clear. YHWH who summons and designates him is firmly resolved that Jeremiah shall do the task. Indeed, YHWH has intended this before his birth. YHWH will not be resisted, and the prophet is compelled, even though his work will be high risk. YHWH promises to protect him in the midst of the threats he will face. This tense interaction may be parsed in two ways: first as the personal struggle of the prophet, but second as evidence of how abruptly unwelcome is the intrusion of

YHWH into the public sphere of Jerusalem. Such intrusion exposes the Jerusalem arrangement of power and wealth as unsustainable. In the end the accent is not on the person of Jeremiah but on the word that must be spoken and that will have its public say in the face of entrenched resistance.

This account of prophetic authorization reaches its culmination in 1:10, in which YHWH gives to Jeremiah the thematic substance of his work. Indeed, it can be observed that everything in the book of Jeremiah amounts to an exposition of the sum of verse 10. In this verse we can see that the prophetic task consists of two parts. On the one hand, the prophet has a *negative deconstructive task* that is voiced in four verbs: pluck up, tear down, destroy, overthrow. The imagery is of a violent assault that effects an end to a settled society. The first verb, "tear down," is an architectural term. It refers to the razing of a building or a wall. The second term, "pluck up," is agricultural. It concerns uprooting plants or destroying a field or a garden. It will be noted, moreover, that the prophetic assignment is not simply to report on such actions, but to perform them by utterance in a way that penetrates and puts under threat the ideology that legitimates the social structures and arrangements that seem so secure. Prophetic speech itself has a decisive impact on social reality, which of course is why every dominant regime wants to silence prophetic speech. These next two verbs, "destroy" and "overthrow," add to the rhetorical intensity of the negative charge.

The second task of the prophet is voiced in the last two verbs of 1:10, "build" and "plant," in turn an architectural and then an agricultural image. Thus "build" is a match for "tear down," and "plant" is a counterpoint for "pluck up." Thus the prophetic task is not only one of dismantling but also, on the other hand, has *a second task of construction and restoration.* To use more familiar language, the two tasks are *divine judgment* and *divine restoration.* In the positive as in the negative, the prophet is not only to speak of planting and building, but to perform such acts by utterance—that is, to generate new social possibility.

These six verbs thematize the prophetic task and the prophetic book. In the context of ancient Jerusalem the four negative verbs bespeak the end of royal Jerusalem, the end of the dynasty, the razing of the temple, and the nullification of the social, economic, and political enterprise that took itself to be chosen of YHWH. The outcome of this negative articulation in historical fact was the deportation of important members of the community—the abyss of exile. As we have seen, the actual historical event did not match the extravagant rhetoric of the prophet. The reason that the more modest historical happening became decisive for Judaism and for the Bible, however, is that this prophetically proclaimed loss specified the profound fracture of YHWH from Israel. The same disproportion may be noticed between the historical event of 9/11 and its symbolic impact, because that event also specified, amid the "exceptionalism" of the United States, a fracture of its deep ideological claims.

The final two verbs bespeak the restoration of Jerusalem (a "new Jerusalem") with a rebuilt temple and a restored viable economic community. Not to be missed is the fact that the second task also belongs to Jeremiah, even though the weight of the book is on the negative and even though his prophetic reputation as weeping prophet accents the loss. Thus the dual thematic of the book of Jeremiah and the task of the prophet is *displacement and restoration*, both accomplished according to the purpose of YHWH.

These six verbs (with variants) become the oft-repeated leitmotif of the book of Jeremiah:

- In 18:7–10, the verbs recur to indicate that both tasks are in the reach of YHWH's capacity. YHWH, moreover, has complete freedom both to will an action, negative or positive, and to reverse field as YHWH deems appropriate. YHWH's governance, in this text, concerns exactly the work of termination and restoration.

- In 24:7, the text addresses the deported in Babylon and assures them that YHWH's intention now is to build and not tear down, to plant and not pluck up. The verbs anticipate a good future for the exiled.

- In 31:18, the negative task, given in five verbs ("bring evil" is added to the repertoire), has been completed. Now the divine resolve is restoration: "plant and build."

- In 45:4, YHWH resolves to do the harsh negative work. But then in verse 5, Baruch, as the point person for the subcommunity of the faithful, is issued a pass on the destruction wrought by YHWH. The destruction will concern "the whole land," except for those whose life is exempted by YHWH.

This array of texts exhibits the deep, hard work of the prophet. The prophetic task is not to be an advocate on any element of particular public policy. Beneath those matters the prophet addresses the elemental reality of coming to terms with the sheer uncompromising rule of YHWH that will not be mocked or disregarded. While most of the book of Jeremiah concerns the future of Jerusalem and its inhabitants, in 1:10 the prophetic mandate is "over nations and over kingdoms." The rule of YHWH is not circumscribed to Israel or to Jerusalem. The book of Jeremiah has in purview YHWH's rule of all. Note especially the Oracles against the Nations in chapters 46–51, wherein the nations must come to terms with YHWH. In that corpus, moreover, the culminating oracle concerns the kingdom of Babylon that will rise with Nebuchadnezzar as "servant of YHWH" (25:9; 27:6), but then before he finishes Jeremiah anticipates the demise of Babylon as it is torn down and plucked up (51:64). Both accents of 1:10 make their way even to mighty Babylon!

When we read 1:10 toward the New Testament in Christian interpretation, we readily see that the negatives of "pluck up and tear down" figure as *the crucifixion of Jesus* and the positive terms of "plant and build" concern *the resurrection of Jesus*. Thus in Christian parlance what happens to Jerusalem in the Old Testament (displacement and restoration) happens to the person of Jesus, who is *executed* but also *empowered* to new life (John 2:19–22). The God who nullifies what is unacceptable is the God who evokes newness beyond our expectation. So it is for Israel and for the church. In a former time when the church did not flinch from this radical notion of YHWH's governance, the church could sing,

Before Jehovah's awful throne,
Ye nations, bow with sacred joy;
Know that the Lord is God alone,
He can create, and He destroy.[1]

That twofold prophetic mandate is given eloquent expression in the rhetoric of Paul. The prophetic negatives receive this formulation:

God chose what is low and despised in the world, things that are not, to reduce to nothing things that are. (1 Corinthians 1:28)

So Jerusalem is reduced to nothing; so Jesus is in turn reduced to nothing. In the horizon of Paul, the "strong and wise" of the world are brought to nullity. Conversely, the positives of Jeremiah receive this articulation:

in the presence of the God in whom he believed, who gives life to the dead and calls into existence the things that do not exist. (Romans 4:17)

In the narrative of the Old Testament, God called into existence a new Jerusalem and a new covenant. In Christian formulation, in Easter God called into existence the new rule of Christ beyond Friday. And now in the world, God is calling into newness social reality beyond our imagination. All of this is entrusted to the prophet. It is no wonder Jeremiah tried to refuse the mandate, a brief that puts all of life beyond our control.

Questions for Discussion

1. What do you make of the six commissioning verbs found in Jeremiah 1?

2. How do you see Jeremiah's call as risky?

3. Where else do you see echoes of Jeremiah's call showing up in the New Testament?

4. Have you ever felt God's call? In destructive or restorative modes? Or both?

Chapter 3

No Water!
(Jeremiah 2:13)

For my people have committed two evils:
they have forsaken me,
the fountain of living water,
and dug out cisterns for themselves,
cracked cisterns
that can hold no water.

Scripture Passages for Reference

Exodus 15:22
Exodus 17:1–7
Jeremiah 15:18
Psalm 22:1
Psalm 105:41
John 4:10, 14

Jeremiah 2–20 is often reckoned to be a literary unit. This long section is bracketed at the outset by chapter 1 and the "call narrative" of Jeremiah, and at the end by the prose narrative of chapter 21. In this long sweep of text there is great variation of accents and literary genres. The most prominent note sounded by the prophet, however, consists in what interpreters call the prophetic "speech of judgment." That recurring pattern of speech often includes two elements: an *indictment* that details Israel's wrongdoing and a *judicial sentence* that anticipates the punitive future that Israel will face. These two elements are handled with great dexterity and imagination, but the common intent of such speech is characteristically to articulate what it costs for Israel to live in contradiction to the will of YHWH. Such a way of living, concludes the prophet, can only have a sorry outcome.

In the Old Testament, *atheism*—the conviction that there is no God—is rarely an issue. By contrast, the practice of *idolatry*—worship of a wrong or false god—is an issue that permeates the prophetic texts. In the poetic imagination of the ancient world, such false gods were of course given names. But we should not for that reason conclude that idolatry is simply a "religious" problem. Rather, the worship of a false god inevitably matches the living of a false life, so that idolatry is not only expressed in worship but is also expressed in social conduct that comes with a false god, thus in an anti-neighborly attitude expressed in practice and in policy that is eventually self-destructive. Thus the "speeches of judgment" in Jeremiah 2–20 recurringly assert that Israel has opted for *false gods* that eventuate in *false living* that will in turn eventuate in loss, destruction, and displacement.

From this array of texts in chapters 2–20, I have selected one that we may consider as an epitome of a prophetic speech of judgment (2:13). In the extended poem of 2:5–19, the prophetic indictment declares that Israel "went after worthless things" ("bubbles" and idols) and became as worthless as the idols (2:5). The waywardness of Israel led to a disregard of God (2:6) and of the Torah (2:8). The verdict of 2:11 is that Israel has "changed gods." "My people" Israel had the covenantal commitment of YHWH as their "glory," their identity and ground of well-being in the world, but Israel has traded that "glory" for "no gods" who are powerless and embody shame rather than glory. The exchange is even more astonishing, says the poet, because there has never been another nation so stupid as to make that trade. Israel has given up the God of life in order to cohabit with "no god."

This speech of judgment reaches a judicial sentence in verses 15–19 with the notice that foreign powers ("lions") have plundered the land. The poetry alludes specifically to Egypt (Memphis and Tahpanhes) and mentions Assyria, and Babylon no doubt is implied in context. Thus the prophet makes an amazing connection that *the waywardness of Israel* evokes *plunder by foreign powers.* This connection is possible because YHWH is the Lord of those foreign powers as well. Sandwiched between the indictment of verses 5–11 and the judicial sentence of verses 15–18 is our verse, 2:13.

All of this *alienation* that results in *catastrophe* for Israel is caught in the poignant imagery of our verse. In this verse we have a strong prophetic indictment, but the judicial sentence is implied. Prophetic imagination often proceeds by appeal to image and metaphor as a probing of the elusive thickness of Israel's life with God. In this verse the image is of water. It is crucial for this usage to remember that the Bible is situated in an arid climate where water, essential for life, is scarce. The prophetic indictment is in two parts, "two evils": first, rejection of YHWH, and second, embracing unreliable alternatives. The first indictment is "forsake me." The term "forsake" is familiar to us from Psalm 22:1: "My God, my God, why have you forsaken me?" It is a term used for abandonment of a trustworthy relationship—most poignantly marriage, so that the term serves for divorce. In this usage it is assumed that Israel belonged with YHWH in covenant and now has abandoned both reliance on YHWH and obedience to YHWH. The image is made more urgent by the image of water. YHWH is self-portrayed in this verse as a reliable source of the water that is essential for existence. Already in the wilderness narrative, YHWH had the capacity to bring water from rock (Exodus 17:1–7; see also 15:22–25 and Psalm 105:41). YHWH is the supplier of living water; but here YHWH is not the supplier of water but is, in God's own self, the water of life. In Christian parlance the same imagery is utilized to witness to Jesus as the presence of living water:

> "If you knew the gift of God, and who it is that is saying to you, 'Give me a drink,' you would have asked him, and he would have given you living water. . . . Those who drink of the water that I will give them will never be thirsty. The water that I will give will become in them a spring of water gushing up to eternal life." (John 4:10, 14)

Thus God as living water is on offer to Israel. But God operates in freedom. Those who rely on this water do not control the water supply but receive water as it is given. This means that God does not always conform to Israel's particular expectations. Even Jeremiah himself accuses YHWH of unreliability:

> Truly, you are to me like a deceitful brook,
>   like waters that fail.
>   15:18

Here the image is of a stream that runs dry in a season of drought and so fails to supply water. Jeremiah found YHWH to be an unreliable advocate, even though YHWH had promised to protect him. Israel found reliance on YHWH too risky and too demanding. Israel sought for a more reliable source of sustenance. As we have seen in verse 11, that alternative entailed false gods. In this imagery the alternative was a cistern that Israel had dug for itself. Israel is accused of digging out storage places for water so that Israel could provide and control its own water supply, no longer needing to rely on YHWH. This choice of *cisterns* rather than a *fountain* is a push toward self-sufficiency. Israel did not want to rely on YHWH, did not want to trust YHWH, and did not want to be subject to YHWH. The reason is that YHWH as water is on YHWH's terms, terms that entail commandments concerning holiness, justice for the neighbor, and mercy for the needy. The requirement for such water of life is too much!

It would be relatively easy to dig a cistern and control the water on one's own terms. That would make unnecessary trust in YHWH. It would render unnecessary obedience to YHWH and so scuttle the burden of the commandments that require holiness and justice. Life is so much easier if we can control the water of life for ourselves, by the domestication of our religious imagination, by our economic shrewdness, by our military prowess, and by our technological acumen.

The problem noticed by the poet, however, is that cisterns leak. Indeed, from my own experience with cisterns, I judge that it is not possible to dig a cistern that finally does not leak. And if the cistern leaks, the certain outcome is "no water." The phrase "no water" is the stunning conclusion of our verse. For all of Israel's desperate autonomy, "no water" is a death sentence in an arid climate. When Israel depends on its own water supply and that water supply leaks away as cisterns surely will do, Israel will be without water and will die. The phrase "no water" is reminiscent of the past experience of

Israel when it left Egypt and entered the wilderness (see Exodus 15:22). In that instance the only thing that secured the life of Israel was the capacity and willingness of YHWH, via Moses, to inexplicably provide water. But now in Jeremiah, YHWH has been abandoned and Israel is left to its own failing resources.

This prophetic utterance contains no judicial sentence. Such a sentence—a death sentence—is clearly implied. Israel's self-sufficiency will inescapably lead to Israel's expiration. This is no alternative once YHWH has been abandoned as the only source of living water. The poet, as every poet, invites us to linger in the imagery. When we do so, the "fountain of living water" is telling indeed, as the self-sufficient cisterns of leaking water are more ominous. The poet does not even summon Israel to reconsider reliance on YHWH. The image lingers, in its own compelling force, before the dread lure of self-sufficiency.

Questions for Discussion

1. What is a bigger problem in today's world: atheism or idolatry?

2. How do false gods lead to false lives? Are false lives proof of false gods?

3. What are some examples of water "on God's terms"?

4. What are some examples of broken cisterns today?

Chapter 4

Return to Me
(Jeremiah 3:12)

Return faithless Israel,
        says the LORD.
I will not look on you in anger,
    for I am merciful,
        says the LORD;
I will not be angry forever.

Scripture Passages for Reference
Jeremiah 3:12–4:4
Jeremiah 24:4
Deuteronomy 24:1–4
Hosea 2:19–20

Amid the "speeches of judgment" in Jeremiah 2–20 there are also some remarkable rhetorical disruptions to that speech pattern. Among the most interesting of these disruptions is the poetry of 3:12–4:4. (We will for now disregard the prose verses that stand outside the movement of the poetry.) These poetic verses offer the utterance of YHWH and are dominated by a fourfold pattern of a summons (invitation?) for Israel to return to YHWH:

Return, faithless Israel,
    says the LORD.
        3:12

> Return, O faithless children,
>   says the LORD.
>   3:14
>
> Return, O faithless children.
>   3:22
>
> If you return, O Israel,
>   says the LORD,
> if you return to me . . .
>   4:1

The repeated summons affirms that Israel has been wayward and "went far from me" (2:5). These verses can only be understood when they are read in the context of 3:1:

> If a man divorces his wife
>   and she goes from him
> and becomes another man's wife,
>   will he return to her?
> Would not such a land be greatly polluted?

As we will see, the implied answers to these questions (in light of the Torah that Jeremiah knew so well) are: *No*, he will not return to her; *yes*, the land would be greatly polluted. This opening verse of the chapter appeals to an old commandment of Moses in Deuteronomy 24. In that Torah provision it is prescribed that if a man divorces a woman and that woman goes to marry another man who then also divorces her, the woman cannot return to her first husband. She cannot do so if she wants to return; she cannot do so even if the first husband wants her back. The reason she cannot return to him is that contact with the second husband has "defiled" her and made her ritually impure for her first husband.

> For that would be abhorrent [an abomination!] to the LORD, and you shall not bring guilt on the land that the LORD your God is giving you as a possession. (24:4)

This strict provision is the reason that attacking strongmen in the Near East, even now, rape the wives of those whom they attack; such rape makes the women ineligible for their husbands.

Jeremiah 3:1 is a poetic reiteration of the commandment of Moses in Deuteronomy 24:1–4. In the poem, YHWH is cast as the first husband and Israel as the wife. (The imagery is unapologetically patriarchal.) Israel, the wife, has deserted her first husband YHWH and has gone to a second husband, another god. According to the commandment of Moses, she cannot return to YHWH, for she has been "ruined" for that relationship. By appeal to the old commandment, Jeremiah has established a baseline for the poetry that follows. Israel is "ruined" for a relationship with YHWH.

Given the prohibition of the old commandment, this fourfold summons to return in 3:12–4:4 is shocking. It would have been enough to have YHWH urge Israel to return to covenantal fidelity. But with 3:1 as a backdrop, the summons is a surprise and a scandal. The shift from 3:1 that reiterates the Torah commandment to the summons of 3:12 shows that YHWH does a radical reversal in which YHWH is willing and ready to violate the old Torah for the sake of the relationship. YHWH is not contained within the old Torah regulations; YHWH's yearning for this relationship overrides the covenant prohibition that YHWH, via Moses, had asserted after Sinai. YHWH is willing to violate YHWH's own commandment!

This appeal by YHWH to wayward fickle Israel to return is inescapably filled with pathos; it is the voice of a wounded, yearning lover. In the first three appeals (3:11, 14, 22), Israel is described as "faithless." In the Hebrew there is a play on words. The imperative to return is *shuv*. The adjective "faithless" is a participial of the same verb. Israel is "turning"—that is, turning away from YHWH. The imperative to "return" is a bid that Israel should reverse field from *turning away from* to *turning back toward fidelity*.

In 3:12 the ground for the divine summons to return is the assurance that YHWH is a God of fidelity (*ḥesed*) who continues in covenantal fidelity even when Israel does not. This assurance of divine fidelity (NRSV: "merciful") is bracketed by two comments about divine anger: "I will not look on you in anger. . . . I will not be angry forever." This second phrase echoes the assurance of Psalm 103:9. God's fidelity sets a time limit on God's anger toward fickle Israel. After the anger is spent, divine fidelity persists.

In the second summons of 3:14 the imperative is reiterated. Israel is again characterized as fickle. But now the ground of the appeal is YHWH's declaration "I am your master." Remarkably, the word "master" translates the Hebrew *Ba'al*, which is also the name of a rival Canaanite deity, the one who makes things fertile and so gives an heir and thus a future. The use of the term is clever because the imagery of 3:1 alludes to seeking other lovers—that is, other gods in order to receive a future. No, insists YHWH. I am your *Ba'al*. I am the God you are seeking. You do not need to lust after other gods in order to have a future. Indeed, the remainder of verse 14 is a promise that YHWH will bring displaced Israel back to Jerusalem for a future with hope (see 29:11). Thus YHWH will be Israel's future-creating God.

In the third summons (3:22) we have the same imperative and again a characterization of Israel as fickle. Now God promises to heal Israel's fickleness. YHWH has been Israel's "healer" since the exodus (Exodus 15:26). Israel is afflicted with the diseases of Egypt, and YHWH will overcome those pathologies. Those diseases perhaps include greed, fear, and self-centeredness. The use of the word "heal" suggests that Israel's waywardness is pathological addiction. The lust for a different god, a "better" god, is a fearful urge that is a disaster for a covenantal people. YHWH, in YHWH's eagerness for a restored relationship, will override that addiction. Jeremiah 3:22–23 concludes with an acknowledgment voiced by Israel that YHWH is indeed Israel's source of well-being and that the other gods are a delusion (v. 23). This response suggests a readiness by Israel to reengage the covenant.

The fourth use of the same verb in 4:1 now sets the terms of restoration of covenant. The return is an act of YHWH's deep graciousness. But it is not cheap grace! A return is possible only if Israel is prepared to live by the terms that properly belong to YHWH's will and character. The return requires that Israel must forgo practices that are inimical to YHWH (abomination). These surely are the idolatries of greed, fear, and self-centeredness. In place of these seductions the covenant to which Israel may return is marked by *truth* (= reliability), *justice,* and *righteousness*. These are the terms of the old covenantal tradition from which Israel had long since departed. They are already the terms of "marriage" in the imagination of Hosea a century before Jeremiah:

> I will take you for my wife forever; I will take you for my wife in *righteousness* and in *justice*, in *steadfast love,* and in *mercy.* I will take you for my wife in *faithfulness;* and you shall know the LORD. (Hosea 2:19–20)

This fourth unit of the poem concludes with the three other imperatives that are nonnegotiable for the relationship: "break up," "circumcise," "remove" (4:3–4). Israel's acknowledgment in 3:22–23 leaves Israel with much serious work to do in order to act out its affirmation of YHWH.

This remarkable poem is an astonishing disclosure of the reality of the two parties to this relationship. Concerning Israel, the poem shows that Israel has completely forgotten its true character as YHWH's covenant people. This "forgetting" is a primary story line of the Bible (see Psalm 106). But the poetry also asserts that Israel does not need to continue to be such a disordered community, alienated from its true destiny. Even in the dangerous context of displacement, Israel, via this poem, has an opportunity to recover its true character and identity.

In a parallel way, this poetry also articulates YHWH in a fresh way just at a crucial moment in the life of Israel. In that moment, when Jerusalem is under threat and Israel is at risk, it is declared that the God of *uncompromising covenantal requirements* is at the same time a God of *pathos-filled yearning* for a restored covenantal life with Israel. It is exactly the work of the poet to probe the internal emotional life of the Holy One of Israel. Indeed, it is the work of the poet to imagine YHWH out beyond old stereotypes and to show us that the God of Israel, at the very moment of risk, is a God of healing, transformative covenantal fidelity. This God, so the poet dares to say, is willing to put old Torah requirements on hold for the sake of a life of reliable fidelity.

Questions for Discussion

1. Where else does God prove willing to violate God's own commandments?

2. How have God's people alienated themselves from their true destiny, back in the time of Jeremiah or here and now?

3. How does a poem—or Scripture more generally—help us recover our true character and identity?

4. Does this poem in Jeremiah 3 help you imagine God beyond your prior imaginings? How so?

Chapter 5

Not (Yet) a Full End
(Jeremiah 4:27)

*For thus says the L*ORD*: The whole land shall be a desolation;*
yet I will not make a full end.

Scripture Passages for Reference

Jeremiah 4:23-26
Jeremiah 45:4
Genesis 1

Since the book of Jeremiah is headed toward the abyss of exile (1:3), and since God's first work in Jerusalem is to pluck up and tear down, it is not a surprise that Jeremiah speaks frequently about the disaster that is sure to come upon the city. He not only speaks of it frequently, but he does so in a rich variety of images. He speaks of marital infidelity (3:1), stupidity (4:22; 8:7), terminal illness (30:12), foreign invasion (5:15), rotted underwear (13:10), and broken pottery (19:10). The reason he must be so inventive in his speech is that his listeners in Jerusalem were cocooned in an ideology that provided assurance that the city of Jerusalem was protected by God and therefore immune from threat. This ideology permitted Jerusalem to disregard the realities of its life. Thus Jeremiah's rich imagery is an attempt to penetrate that self-deceiving ideology to confront his listeners with a reality check concerning the outcome of living in contradiction to YHWH.

In the tightly disciplined poem of 4:23–26 the poet ups the ante with surprisingly tensive rhetoric. Heretofore the coming disaster that he anticipates has been voiced in terms of historical or everyday experience. But now the rhetoric opens to cosmic scope in which the poet imagines that the perfidy of Israel will have cosmic consequences. The poem features the opening clause "I looked" four times. From the outset YHWH had tested Jeremiah's capacity for sight: "'What do you see?'" (1:11, 13). The prophet is one who can see beyond the capacity of his contemporaries to see the acting out of God's work in the world. The fourfold formula in 4:23–26 each time yields a surprise: "Behold!" That term is rendered in the NRSV as "lo," but the word suggests an exclamation of amazement, because the prophet sees what he had not expected to see. What he sees that surprises him is the dismantling of creation. He first sees that the lights of heaven (sun, moon, stars) had been extinguished (see Genesis 1:16–18). The phrase "waste and void" is a deliberate reference back to Genesis 1:1 ("formless void") that characterizes chaos before God had done God's creative work. The poet observes the created order falling back into originary disorder. Second, he sees that the mountains and hills, the landscape of creation, was destabilized so that the "dry land" (earth) was no longer a viable habitat for creaturely life (see Genesis 1:9–13). Third, he sees that every living creature (human persons and birds) are all gone, thus the negation of the birds of Genesis 1:20 and the loss of human habitation (see Genesis 1:26–27). And fourth, he sees that the created earth designed by the creator to produce abundant fruit trees and green plants is terminated (Genesis 1:29–30).

The poem does nothing less than trace out the dismantling of creation in a point-by-point echo of the Genesis creation narrative. Through Genesis 1 the Bible opens with the dramatic act of God's establishment of a baseline of a reliable, generative created order of abundance that will sustain all creatures in well-being. But of course that created order of abundance is not, in biblical perspective, autonomous. It is not self-sustaining but depends at every instant on the attentive governance of the creator. If the creator were to have a lapse of attentiveness, the entire world would promptly collapse. But of course the creator God is fully faithful and reliable so that the earth can flourish. Its plants and animals can prosper, and human creatures can luxuriate in the abundance of the generative created order.

But now the poet thinks the unthinkable and says the unsayable. He imagines, in this poetic scenario, that the creator's attentive maintenance of the created order has collapsed. It has collapsed, moreover, not because of divine negligence but because God is no longer willing to sustain a created order that lives in defiant rebellion to God's will for creation. The pivot of that defiant rebellion, in the horizon of Jeremiah, is exactly in Jerusalem, where God's own beloved people Israel, in their recalcitrant stupidity, contradict the creator. The poet brings to speech what he discerns to be the exhaustion of God's passion for Jerusalem and consequently for the earth. The poet manages to take the *specific crisis* of recalcitrant Israel and give it *cosmic articulation*. What happens in Jerusalem does not stay in Jerusalem but reaches to the ends of the earth. The reach of recalcitrant Jerusalem causes the undoing of the entire creation!

This fourfold "sighting" of uncreation culminates in verse 26 with identification of the unmistakable agent of uncreation. All of this destruction happens "before the LORD." The creation is occupied with "fierce anger" at the systemic defiance of Jerusalem.

This fourfold utterance is a remarkable act of prophetic imagination. It is, to be sure, only a poem; it is not a scientific diagnosis. The poem is a bid that Jeremiah's Jerusalem listeners might sense the gravity of their waywardness. It will be clear that Jeremiah speaks in the idiom of biblical faith. He does not view the world as a "natural order," but as creation that is reliant upon and accountable to the creator. The world as God's creation is precarious and depends on fidelity for durability. It is of course possible, without much imagination, to transpose this imaginative act into our own current climate crisis. There is no doubt that our crisis also emerges because of greedy predation and undisciplined consumption that refuse to take into account the limits God has ordained in God's created order. When those limits are willfully defied and disregarded long enough, chaos (that always lurks close at hand) is ready to make its assault—in this case a decisive assault.

All of this brings us to 4:27, which is, in context, a rhetorical disruption. It is clear that by the end of verse 26 we have reached the emotional limit of poetic imagination and the poem cannot go further. As a result, verse 27 is quite unexpected. This verse is tiny and innocent-looking, so one might not think it is pivotal for the book of Jeremiah. It is, moreover, a verse of prose after words of daring poetry, so it is something of a letdown. The verse does not seem to fit in context, but there it is. It is fashionable among critics to dismiss the verse as a "gloss" that has been added by later scribes. But there it is. If it is a later gloss, it might have been due to a later (after Jeremiah) awareness that Israel's life and the life of the world did not end as the poem had imagined and so a correction had to be made. Or if it is late (after Jeremiah), perhaps it is a pastoral gesture to soften the unbearable harshness of the preceding lines. Such explanations of a gloss render this wee verse innocuous, to be safely disregarded.

But what if instead of dismissal of the verse we take it as revelatory of God's own propensity? What might it disclose to us after the relentless harshness of verses 23–26? Might it show that after God's rant in verses 23–26, albeit articulated in exquisite poetic fashion, the God whose words these are takes a deep breath? In that moment of a deep breath the Holy One of Israel reverses field. The first part of the verse echoes the preceding: the "whole land" will be destroyed. The same phrase is used in 45:4. (In both uses it might be rendered "the whole earth.") But then the dismayed creator God utters an adversative "yet." (The same turn happens in 45:5 wherein Baruch is excepted from "the whole land.") Here also there is such an exemption. The last phrase is a check on the creator's negative resolve. It is as though the creator, in a shocking moment of self-awareness, recognizes that God's own self cannot act on the preceding verses to perform terminal harshness. God will not do completely what God has said. God will not terminate the earth, the people, or the land. This is the sort of awareness and the sort of reversal of field that every parent knows who has ever erupted in anger toward a beloved child. There is nothing about the land or the people to evoke this adversative "yet." The ground is only in the will and fidelity of the creator, who finally will check "fierce anger" before it is enacted. This check on divine anger is an echo of the same affirmation in 3:12: "I will not be angry forever." This astonishing utterance appears, in this instant, to be a *novum* in the self-awareness of YHWH.

This "yet" that curbs divine anger is indeed a pivotal moment in the life of God, in the life of Israel, and in the life of the book of Jeremiah. This pivotal turn of rhetoric asserts that the God of all faithfulness does not will the end. It is this "yet" that is the ground of Judaism through the troubled vagaries of human history. It is this divine resolve that keeps open futures and makes a way out of no way. This "yet" is the ground, in the Christian gospel, of Easter possibility. This "yet" is the ground for the care of the earth in the face of the climate crisis, not an invitation to complacency for a presumably protected and "inviolable" planet but a summons to active engagement in and for the future. This wee word opens fresh scenarios for the work of Jeremiah, work that has not been voided by the harsh utterances that the poet was required to speak. That "yet" was for Jeremiah a venturesome utterance. And for the creator it constitutes venturesome fidelity.

Questions for Discussion

1. How has our own society become cocooned in an ideology that prevents us from seeing reality?

2. How is seeing reality achieved?

3. Does "recalcitrant stupidity" always "contradict the creation" in your judgment?

4. Can you imagine God being exhausted with God's people and creation?

Chapter 6

The All-Important "If"
(Jeremiah 7:6–7)

If you do not oppress the alien, the orphan, and the widow, or shed innocent blood in this place, and if you do not go after other gods to your own hurt, then I will dwell with you in this place, in the land that I gave of old to your ancestors forever and ever.

Scripture Passages for Reference

Jeremiah 7:1–8:3
Jeremiah 26:4–14
Exodus 19:6
Deuteronomy 24:1
1 Kings 9:4–7
Psalm 78

Amid the dazzling, demanding poetry of Jeremiah 2–20, 7:1–8:3 stands out as a most important prose passage. The text is commonly termed Jeremiah's "temple sermon." It is an oration presented "at the gate of the LORD's house"—that is, in front of the temple in Jerusalem. This location indicates that Jeremiah takes a public stand where he is sure to be heard and noticed by all the important people in Jerusalem, among them priests and the king. This is indeed *truth* speaking to *power*. The text is termed a "sermon," I suppose, because it is a hortatory exposition that aims at the embrace of serious trust and obedience.

The core of Jeremiah's message in this "sermon" is in verses 5–7. These verses include an "if" four times (two in Hebrew). This usage indicates that YHWH's covenant loyalty toward Israel depends on Israel keeping its part of the covenant agreement through adherence to YHWH's commandments. In this strand of biblical testimony, YHWH's covenant is conditional; such conditionality, moreover, means that the covenant can be placed in jeopardy and terminated. Such a take on covenant is reflective of the thought of the tradition of Deuteronomy. And behind Deuteronomy it goes all the way back to the Sinai covenant, where the "if" of conditionality is articulated: "'Now therefore, if you obey my voice and keep my covenant, you shall be my treasured possession out of all the peoples'" (Exodus 19:5). The condition of covenant is to "obey my voice" and "keep my covenant."

Jeremiah's usage of the "if" begins in our verses broadly and then has two quite specific elements. The first "if" is an appeal for "amendment" (repentance). The second "if" is a general mandate on justice. But the third "if" makes the mandate of justice quite specific; it pertains to outsiders, orphans, and widows. This triad of the vulnerable is an old formulation from the tradition of Deuteronomy (16:11; 24:17, 19–24). It is a catalog of those without an advocate in a patriarchal society. Outsiders (immigrants) have no natural advocate. Orphans are without advocating fathers, and widows are without protective husbands. Thus the covenantal community is mandated to provide advocacy for those who have no "normal" advocates and who are for that reason most vulnerable in a predatory economy. The words of Jeremiah echo the Torah: "You shall not deprive a *resident alien* or an *orphan* of justice; you shall not take a *widow*'s garment in pledge" (Deuteronomy 24:17). This "if" is a form of *loving one's neighbor*, with an insistence that the immigrant, orphan, and widow are indeed our neighbors.

The fourth "if" prohibits idolatry and by tacit implication insists on adherence only to the holy God of covenant. Thus it is a mandate to love the Lord your God with all your heart. In sum, these conditions of covenant amount to loving neighbor and loving God.

The four uses of "if" in our text concerning Torah conditionality are followed by a "then" in Jeremiah 7:7. This "then"—the consequence of following the mandates of YHWH—is that YHWH will be present in "this place." The verse itself suggests that "this place" is the land of promise that without the presence of YHWH would not be filled with abundant life for Israel. But the context suggests that "this place" is more particularly Jerusalem and perhaps even more particularly the temple in Jerusalem. Performance of the mandates makes it possible for YHWH to be present among the people of the covenant!

It is worth pondering this if-then rhetoric because it provides assurance that the covenant to which Jeremiah bears witness is transactional; YHWH's faithfulness is dependent upon Israel's faithfulness. The negative counterpoint in this rhetoric is not voiced but is clearly implied. If Israel does not heed this mandate, then YHWH will not be present in Israel. The rhetoric of "if-then" is familiar in the tradition of Deuteronomy. The negative if-then is not often given voice, but we may notice it in 1 Kings 9:4–7, where both the positive and the negative are symmetrically articulated:

> "*If* you will walk before me, as David your father walked, with integrity of heart and uprightness, doing according to all that I have commanded you, and keeping my statutes and my ordinances, *then* I will establish your royal throne over Israel forever." (vv. 4–5)

> "*If* you turn aside from following me, you or your children, and do not keep my commandments and my statutes that I have set before you, but go and serve other gods and worship them, *then* I will cut off Israel from the land." (vv. 6–7)

It will be a surprise to some that the covenant is conditional and transactional, but that is the rhetoric that emerges when strong moral passion heats up. As we will see later on in the book of Jeremiah itself, this tight logic of "if-then" cannot be sustained in dire circumstance. In exile when Israel was extremely vulnerable, YHWH found it necessary to move beyond this logic to self-giving gracious embrace. Thus the book of Jeremiah (and the Bible more generally) moves agilely between *transactional conditionality* and *unconditional graciousness* from God. But then that is exactly the way of our effective parenting. We exercise firm discipline with our children in a rigorous if-then; such rigor, however, is sometimes suspended in something like unconditional love from parents. Good parenting perforce entails both maneuvers. It turns out that good covenanting requires the same.

In our chapter Jeremiah can go on to imagine the enactment of the negative implication of his if-then logic. He invites his listeners to reflect on Shiloh (v. 12), an ancient sanctuary of Israel that was devastated by the Philistines and long ago was left in ruins; his listeners would have remembered that ancient site, now a perpetual ruin without any possibility of a future. The daring move of Jeremiah is to imagine that even the beloved holy city of Jerusalem could be reduced to ruins if the Torah is not honored. Such an analogy would have been scandalous to his hearers and surely bordered on treason for the political leadership.

In Psalm 78, a song likely used in temple liturgy, Jerusalem was celebrated as a positive alternative to rejected Shiloh:

> He abandoned his dwelling at Shiloh,
>   the tent where he dwelt among mortals.
> ....
> But he chose the tribe of Judah,
>   Mount Zion, which he loves.
> He built his sanctuary like the high heavens,
>   like the earth, which he has founded forever.
>   Psalm 78:60, 68–69

While Shiloh was rejected by YHWH, Jerusalem was chosen by God. Now Jeremiah rejects the statement of *contrast* between the two and evokes a *similarity*: Jerusalem will receive the same future as did Shiloh. Jerusalem gets no pass and has no guarantee. Jerusalem is subject to the rigors of Torah obedience. In this utterance, Jeremiah upends the ideology of Jerusalem's exceptionalism; he does so with an insistence that Jerusalem is at risk because what counts is not temple ideology but Torah obedience. The analogue to Shiloh is as daring as if one could imagine making Washington, D.C., or New York City not unlike Hiroshima. And of course the assault on our cities on 9/11 evokes exactly such awareness among us, placing in jeopardy the sense of exceptionalism on which our national ideology rests.

It is no wonder that Jeremiah's words evoked aggressive hostility from establishment powers that had a great stake in the ideology of exceptionalism. In Jeremiah 26, a companion piece to Jeremiah 7, the core of his sermon is reiterated with the same if-then rhetoric:

> *If* you will not listen to me, to walk in my law that I have set before you, and to heed the words of my servants the prophets whom I send to you urgently—though you have not heeded—*then* I will make this house like Shiloh, and I will make this city a curse for all the nations of the earth. (26:4–6)

The religious leadership (priests and prophets) brought charges of treason against Jeremiah in response, because he had uttered the unutterable:

> "You shall die! Why have you prophesied in the name of the LORD, saying, 'This house shall be like Shiloh, and this city shall be desolate, without inhabitant'?" (vv. 8–9)

Jeremiah is on trial for his life with a charge of treason. The narrative goes on to report that in a near-run case, Jeremiah is rescued by two interventions in the trial that seems to be on its way to a death sentence. First, he is rescued by an *appeal to prophetic precedent* that shows the legitimacy of prophetic critique of the establishment ideology. Village elders remembered that their local prophet, Micah, had, a century earlier, anticipated the destruction of Jerusalem:

> Therefore because of you
> Zion shall be plowed as a field;
> Jerusalem shall become a heap of ruins,
> and the mountain of the house a wooded height.
> Micah 3:12 (see Jeremiah 26:18)

This is a remarkable instance of the Bible quoting the Bible. The poetic words of the prophet Micah have lingered and have not lost their force; his words still have compelling authority among those who have not succumbed to royal ideology. This citation of old poetry evidenced the legitimacy of the words of Jeremiah that sounded so much like treason to his contemporaries.

Second, we are told that the *politically powerful family* of Shaphan moved to protect the prophet in his time of trial: "But the hand of Ahikam son of Shaphan was with Jeremiah so that he was not given over into the hands of the people to be put to death" (26:24).

In the book of Jeremiah, Shaphan and his son and his grandson constitute a powerful force in Jerusalem politics that had not accepted royal ideology and that regarded royal policy as foolish and self-destructive. They supported Jeremiah in his daring utterance. This indicates that the prophet was not a loner but was a spokesperson for a political following that refused and resisted official Jerusalem policy. The burden of Jeremiah's sermon is that a public enterprise that contradicts YHWH's intent cannot secure itself and will, sooner or later, be in jeopardy. This is a truth that all the illusion of an ideology of exceptionalism cannot override.

Questions for Discussion

1. Where else do you see the if-then dynamic in Scripture? In the world? Might it apply also to the Christian church? How so?

2. What do you make of the conditional-unconditional dynamic found in Scripture more generally?

3. Do you see an ideology of exceptionalism today? Where? How might it be challenged?

Chapter 7

No Peace
(Jeremiah 8:11)

They have treated the wound of my people carelessly,
saying "Peace, peace,"
when there is no peace.

Scripture Passages for Reference

Jeremiah 8:9–12
Jeremiah 30:12–15
1 Samuel 7:16
1 Kings 8:12–13
Psalm 46

The Jerusalem that Jeremiah inhabited was in a deep even if unacknowledged crisis, heading toward the abyss of exile. The power people in the city lived inside an ideology that was remote from social, economic, and political reality. As a result the city (and therefore the state) functioned according to self-deception and illusion. The ideology that became the dominant narrative of the city has its roots in memories of the two great kings, David and Solomon. On the one hand, David had received a stunning unconditional promise from YHWH that was a perpetual assurance to the dynasty:

Your house and your kingdom shall be made sure forever before
me; your throne shall be established forever. (2 Samuel 7:16)

Inside that memory it was impossible to imagine that the dynasty
or its rule could ever be under threat. On the other hand, the temple
built by King Solomon was taken to be the permanent residence of
YHWH so that YHWH would, perforce, be the durable patron and
guarantor of the temple and the city:

"The LORD has said that he would dwell in thick darkness.
I have built you an exalted house,
    a place for you to dwell in forever."

1 Kings 8:12–13

This dual guarantee to the Jerusalem establishment, moreover,
was confirmed a century before Jeremiah when the city was inexplicably (miraculously!) rescued from the ominous threat of the Assyr-
ian army under Sennacherib:

"For I will defend this city to save it, for my own sake and for the
sake of my servant David." (Isaiah 37:35)

It is popularly thought that Psalm 46, a song no doubt utilized in the
liturgy of the Jerusalem temple, may be a liturgical celebration of
that wondrous deliverance:

There is a river whose streams make glad the city of God,
    the holy habitation of the Most High.
God is in the midst of the city; it shall not be moved;
    God will help it when the morning dawns.

Psalm 46:4–5

All of these traditions together generate and maintain a conviction
that the city is guaranteed and cannot face any serious threat. Such a
conviction would of course deliver the power people from any incon-
venient moral obligation.

The tag word for the ideology of throne and temple is the word
shalom. While we translate it as "peace," the term more broadly
bespeaks security, well-being, and a healthy prosperous social
order. The word *shalom* is included as part of the name of the city—
Jeru-*salem* (see Genesis 14:18)—and the great king of the city,

Solomon, has a name derived from it; he is taken to be as an embodiment of *shalom* (see 2 Samuel 12:14; 1 Kings 10:7–9). All of this together made *shalom* a summary of the claims, hopes, and illusions of the city's power structure.

That ideology of *shalom* was increasingly remote from lived reality. If one could escape the thralldom of that ideology, one was able to see that the city-state of Jerusalem was in fact under internal threat because of economic exploitation that generated a wealth gap between the haves and have-nots. As we have seen, King Jehoiakim is chided by Jeremiah for exploitation of workers. Eventually an alert observer could also see that the ambition of the Babylonian kings constituted an external threat against Israel. Babylon had commercial ambitions, and Israel stood in its way. The internal economic threat and the external military threat together put the city-state in great jeopardy. It was only the immense force of the king-temple ideology of *shalom* that allowed the leaders in Jerusalem to ignore Israel's acute jeopardy.

Into that toxic distance between ideology and reality comes the work of Jeremiah. As we have seen, Jeremiah is grounded in the rural village of Anathoth, which has an edgy relationship with Jerusalem ideology. He will have no part of that ideology, and for that reason he has the capacity to see clearly what his Jerusalem contemporaries are unable and unwilling to see.

Our text is a prophetic address to the managers, advocates, and beneficiaries of that ideology. These prophetic words call Israel out of that ideology to see reality as the prophet sees it, without the distorting lens of ideology. We can notice that 8:9–12 is a wondrously crafted poem. It begins in verse 9 with an identification of the "wise"—those well-placed, well-connected people who have the greatest stake in the ideology and who will be put to shame. The humiliation they will suffer is that "conquerors" (specifically the Babylonians) will seize their fields and their wives. The poem uses a word pair already operative in the Tenth Commandment, "Do not covet your *neighbor's field* or your *neighbor's wife*" (Exodus 20:17). They will be humiliated when they recognize that their ideology did not protect them at all. They will see the consequences of their greed. The rhetoric of the prophet addresses the entire power structure of the urban elites. None of them is exempted. Their greed has propelled them into self-destructive conduct.

The theme is reiterated in verse 12. The leadership is indicted for its shameless way of living. The *shamelessness* in verse 12 links to the *shame* of verse 9. They have no moral compass and therefore no capacity to be embarrassed by their actions or policies. The "therefore" of verse 12 echoes the "therefore" in verse 10, both of which trace out the consequences of shamelessness that violates both common decency (therefore foolishness) and the will of YHWH. The sum and depth of that violation is the term "abomination," an act disgusting because it contradicts YHWH's will for YHWH's creation. Thus in verses 9–10 and in verse 12, the poem *indicts* and then *sentences* the power structure of prophets, priests, and the wise for their obdurate stance that is made possible and credible (required!) by their ideology.

Sandwiched between the "speech of judgment" in verses 9–10 and its reiteration in verse 12 is our verse 11. This verse concerns "they," a reference back to prophets, priests, and the wise, surely scribes and kings as well—that is, the political, religious, and learned leadership of the city. The "wound of my people" refers to the disorder of injustice and exploitation that generated an economy in which an oligarchy of wealth preyed upon hapless peasants and made common life unlivable. Elsewhere Jeremiah can speak of the "wound" in both sorrow and resignation:

> For the hurt of my poor people I am hurt,
>   I mourn, and dismay has taken hold of me.
> > 8:21

> Your hurt is incurable,
>   your wound is grievous.
> There is no one to uphold your cause,
>   no medicine for your wound,
>   no healing for you.
> . . . .
>   Your pain is incurable.
> > 30:12–13, 15

The pounding insistence of 30:13 refuses any assurance or relief: *no* one, *no* medicine, *no* healing! The wound is terminal, as is obvious to anyone who looks.

But the power structure of the city has a great vested interest in making sure that no one notices the seriousness of the malady. And so the opinion-makers and propagandists for the establishment are unleashed upon the populace to reiterate the mantra of the ideology. One can imagine both political and religious leaders repeatedly sounding the tag word of David and Solomon, "Shalom, shalom, shalom." It is an ancient anticipation of "Make America great again." Or one can imagine, in the flourishing Israelite (or U.S.) exceptionalism, a crowd gathered in something like the temple square shouting the equivalent of "USA, USA, USA," as though the cry would remedy the sickness when in fact all that it accomplishes is concealment of the crisis from view. Such mass affirmation has no interest in or patience with the facts on the ground. Such a cry of cover-up will not pause to care about economic exploitation, foolish foreign policy, or damage to creation. It is enough to repeat the mantra because the mantra will "disappear" all the risk and danger.

I take the liberty of such contemporaneity because the text seems to require it and because the parallels are inescapable. I do not make these connections in order to have Jeremiah speak to our time and place. Rather my intent is the opposite, that a consideration of our own circumstance may allow us to discern more fully the dramatic impact of Jeremiah's assertion upon his own contemporaries. He conducts an unvarnished and bold critical assault on the much-treasured conviction of Jerusalem concerning its chosen status; a truth-telling poet will not be toned down by such ideology or the force of its proponents.

Thus we may consider the artistic structure of the poem:

- Shame . . . *therefore* (8:9–10)
- Shalom, shalom . . . shalom (v. 11)
- Shame . . . *therefore* (v. 12)

At the center of the poem is a mocking echo of the simplistic mantra on which the power structure relies to abrogate the reality of the risk at hand. In that verse the ultimate verdict at the end is "no peace"—thus a reiteration of "no one, no medicine, no healing" (30:13). None!

The prophet intends to expose the illusion sustained by the mantra in the service of the ideology. Jeremiah must have succeeded enough that his words have been remembered. Indeed, they are reiterated in 6:13–15. This double use of them suggests that the words have immense staying power; various critical voices after Jeremiah came to see the futility of the mantra and all that it implied. These words of Jeremiah constitute a massive refutation of the resignation by King Hezekiah a century earlier when he had sold out to Babylon and was reprimanded by the prophet Isaiah. The feeble response of the king to the prophetic reprimand is "'There will be peace and security in my days'" (Isaiah 39:8).

"Peace and security in my days" is not enough. Jeremiah knows that we cannot run out the clock on shame-filled policy and practice. The mantra is not strong or persuasive enough to cover over the reality of the day. It is such uncompromising reality that evokes this signature utterance of prophetic imagination.

Questions for Discussion

1. What thing/idea/issue is inviolable in your opinion?

2. Is it imaginable that that thing/idea/issue may be violable after all?

3. How do you see Jeremiah's text applicable today? Where is "Peace, peace" uttered now when in truth there is no peace?

Chapter 8

What to Praise?
(Jeremiah 9:23–24)

Do not let the wise boast in their wisdom, do not let the mighty boast in their might, do not let the wealthy boast in their wealth; but let those who boast boast in this, that they understand and know me, that I am the LORD; I act with steadfast love, justice, and righteousness in the earth, for in these things I delight, says the LORD.

Scripture Passages for Reference

Deuteronomy 17:14–20
Psalms 111–112
Matthew 23:23
2 Corinthians 8:9

The prophets of ancient Israel (and certainly Jeremiah) did their imaginative work always in the presence of the power structure of Jerusalem that featured kings, priests, and scribes. It was the work of the prophets (and certainly Jeremiah) to articulate a radical either-or that confronted their listeners with difficult and urgent decisions. This either-or was *either* to embrace the royal-temple ideology that legitimated the power structure of the city, *or* to opt for an ancient covenantal tradition that stood over against and contradicted the claims of Jerusalem ideology.

This text articulates in a most succinct fashion the deep either-or that occupied Jeremiah and the other prophets more generally. On the one side, the option rejected by Jeremiah, there is the celebration of the accoutrements of prestige and influence: "Do not let the wise boast in their wisdom, do not let the mighty boast in their might, do not let the wealthy boast in their wealth."

The word "boast" in Hebrew is *hll*, the root of "hallelujah." That is, do not say "hallelujah" to the wisdom, wealth, or might. Do not admire the wealthy, do not celebrate the wise, do not exalt the powerful. The reason that the prophet speaks negatively of this triad is that these three marks of human achievement repeatedly and characteristically distort social relationships and sooner or later skew the created order.

In the Old Testament these three features of human achievement are most visibly linked to King Solomon. Solomon is celebrated as the ultimately wise king:

> God gave Solomon very great wisdom, discernment, and breadth of understanding as vast as the sand on the seashore, so that Solomon's wisdom surpassed the wisdom of all the people of the east, and all the wisdom of Egypt. (1 Kings 4:29–30; see also 10:6–7, 23–24)

In this usage, "wisdom" features the technical capacity to manage the earth and human resources in clever ways to one's advantage. The narrative of Solomon shows that Solomon's wisdom turned out to be foolishness, as his reign ended in self-destruction in a tax revolt in response to the exploitation of his rule (1 Kings 12:1–19).

Wealth is a marker of Solomon's regime that he acquired by predatory taxation (1 Kings 4:7–19), by tribute (tariffs?), and by cheap coercive labor (5:13–18; 9:20–23). His grandiose temple was an exhibit of his large store of gold that was extravagantly displayed (6:20–22; 7:48–50). It is evident that Solomon had amassed his great wealth at the expense of the vulnerable he readily exploited for his own aggrandizement. Solomon's wealth was an outcome of his might. He was an arms dealer (10:26–29), and he had a line of military fortifications (9:15–19). He had leverage to have his way in the world. We may take King Solomon to be both an embodiment of and a metaphor for the triad that Jeremiah identifies as a betrayal of covenantal faith. Deuteronomy warns against predatory kings of Solomon's ilk and likely has Solomon specifically in purview:

> He [the king] must not acquire many horses for himself, or return the people to Egypt in order to acquire more horses. . . . And he must not acquire many wives for himself, or else his heart will turn away; also silver and gold he must not acquire in great quantity for himself. (Deuteronomy 17:16–17)

This warning precludes the accumulation of horses (armaments), wives (an exhibit of aggressive virility), silver, and gold. Such accumulation, ancient or contemporary, reduces all of life to a collection of commodities. That commoditization of social reality, moreover, can only end in the distortion of all neighborliness.

The other triad that Jeremiah identifies is relational: steadfast love, justice, righteousness. These terms bespeak neighborly interaction in which the common interest of "haves" and "have-nots" is a defining prospect. Steadfast love is a practice of tenacious solidarity whereby covenant commitments are made and kept through which each looks to the interest of the other. Justice concerns the generous distribution of social goods and the guarantee of a viable, safe life with dignity, even for the most vulnerable and those without resources of their own. Righteousness is the practice of social relationships that allow the community to flourish when all give generously to the well-being of all. The three terms bespeak a covenantal relationship in which neighborly solidarity is both a compelling vision and a defining practice. Psalm 111 articulates the way of YHWH in which YHWH practices these commitments:

> He provides food for those who fear him;
> he is ever mindful of his covenant.
> . . . .
> The works of his hands are faithful and just;
> all his precepts are trustworthy.
> Psalm 111:5–7

Psalm 112, a counterpoint to Psalm 111, characterizes the human practice of such a life of neighborliness:

> It is well with those who deal generously and lend,
> who conduct their affairs with justice.
> . . . .

> They have distributed freely, they have given to the poor;
>   their righteousness endures forever;
>   their horn is exalted in honor.
>
> Psalm 112:5, 9

Jeremiah asserts, moreover, that these three qualities of relationship are not only good ideas or humane possibilities. They are the qualities of life that are pleasing to YHWH. Thus YHWH is not only an object to worship or a "nice uncle" with generous gifts. He is one who weighs in on the great public issues that determine how social relationships are ordered and how social goods are produced and distributed. The long recital of covenantal sanctions (blessings and curses) in Deuteronomy 28 makes clear that adherence to or rejection of the preferences of YHWH has profound consequences for the future of a society. This succinct verdict by Jeremiah is not only an ethical teaching; it is a theological probe into the character of YHWH, the ground for taking YHWH seriously, and the cost of disregarding the will of YHWH.

Thus we are given an urgent either-or:

Either: wisdom, wealth, might

Or: steadfast love, justice, righteousness

We can trace this either-or through the Bible. Indeed, the Bible is an insistence that this either-or of *commodity* or *community* is the defining issue in the life of the world. When in Christian tradition this either-or is parsed through Jesus, attention may be paid to 1 Corinthians 1, which culminates in this apostolic urging: "'Let the one who boasts, boast in the Lord'" (1:31).

This conclusion of Paul is a clear reference to our verse in Jeremiah. In 1 Corinthians 1 Paul contrasts the *wisdom of the world* with the *foolishness of Christ* and the *strength (might) of the world* with the *weakness of Christ*. Thus an accent on *wisdom and might (foolishness and weakness)* takes up two elements of Jeremiah's triad. The third one is readily found in 2 Corinthians where Paul declares the *poverty of Christ* is very different from the *wealth of the world*: "For you know the generous act of our Lord Jesus Christ, that though he was rich, yet for your sakes he became poor, so that by his poverty you might become rich" (2 Corinthians 8:9).

Thus Paul's witness to Jesus is a reiteration of Jeremiah's triad, with the conviction that Jesus *fully enacts resistance* to the triad of wisdom, wealth, and might, and *fully embodies* the triad of steadfast love, justice, and righteousness expressed through his foolishness, weakness, and poverty. Jesus unmistakably chose, every time, neighborly community over commodity. The triad of "'justice and mercy and faith'" in Matthew 23:23 is a near reiteration of the same accent. Jesus' call to his disciples is a summons to embrace and live out that alternative triad.

When we read our contemporary social situation through this deep either-or, we have no difficulty seeing its pertinence to us. We live in a society that is deeply fractured by the accumulation of *great wealth* that distorts neighborliness. We live in an economy of *might* wherein the powerful can legally leverage their greedy way about every issue. And we live in a society dominated by the *"wisdom" of technology* that imagines that every human vexation and limitation has a technological "fix," if only we knew more and controlled more. That assumption is a gross miscalculation grounded in a gross misreading of the human situation. It is a miscalculation that brings with it huge costs for human well-being.

Jeremiah invites us to think again about what we will praise, celebrate, and prefer. His urging, reiterated by Jesus, is counterintuitive to the reductions of the "royal" world that characteristically summons us to engage in self-delusion. Embrace of that in which God delights provides a more excellent way in the world!

Questions for Discussion

1. Where do you see wealth, wisdom, and might in a negative way?

2. Where do you see steadfast love, justice, and righteousness now?

3. How are we prone to praise these various things, and how can or ought we do that in better ways?

Chapter 9

Real Idols versus the True Lord
(Jeremiah 10:16)

Not like these is the LORD, the portion of Jacob,
for he is the one who formed all things,
and Israel is the tribe of his inheritance;
the LORD of hosts is his name.

Scripture Passages for Reference

Jeremiah 10:1–14
Isaiah 44:9–20
Psalm 115

The extended poem of 10:1–16 is an oddity in the textual unit of Jeremiah 2–20. While much of this larger unit is in poetry, none of it is like this particular poetry. On the one hand, these verses are different because the subject is idolatry, a theme that is uncommon in Jeremiah. On the other hand, this poem is boldly doxological in its magnification of YHWH. It contains nothing of Jeremiah's usual subjects of prophetic indictment and prophetic sentence. While some interpreters believe that the poem is a misfit for Jeremiah, we may be glad it is here, because it is a welcome, bold staking out of claims for YHWH.

The critique of idolatry is an assault on the religious belief and practice of the nations that Israel is tempted to replicate. The intent of the poem is to expose the idols of the nations (and of Israel) as phonies that have no life and no power. The tone of the expose is ridicule, designed to help those tempted by idols to see how futile they are. The idols are dismissed as human artifacts. The process of their manufacture is given in detail in verses 3–4, 9. These verses have as a close companion piece Isaiah 44:9–20, which traces the production of idols in mocking detail:

> Half of it he burns in the fire; over this half he roasts meat, eats it and is satisfied. He also warms himself and says, "Ah, I am warm, I can feel the fire!" The rest of it he makes into a god, his idol, bows down to it and worships it; he prays to it and says, "Save me, for you are my god!" (44:16-17)

The outcome of such god-production is offered in one of the richest images of the Bible: the idols are "like scarecrows in a cucumber field" (Jeremiah 10:5). They just stand there; they cannot move and cannot speak. They are a worthless delusion that cannot finally be sustained (v. 15). If they cannot move or speak, they surely cannot save. Those who worship such impotent scarecrows, moreover, are stupid and foolish, relying on objects that cannot deliver (vv. 8, 14).

We should not imagine that in the ancient world idol worshipers were religiously naive. They were wrong, but not naive. They did not trust in objects of wood or metal. Rather, they trusted in the imagined forces that such objects signified. In like manner, those who contemporarily engage in idolatry (all of us?) are not religiously naive—wrong, but not naive. Idolatry is the seduction of trusting in imagined forces that cannot deliver. So we may notice that among us the idols that tempt us include nationalism, racism, beauty, youth, or technology in its many forms. None of these is a giver of life that will be safe, joyous, or generative. Such idols have no such gifts to give, even though we continue to trust in them.

It turns out that in the poem these harsh strictures against idols and their worshipers is simply a launching pad for testimony about YHWH. YHWH is unlike the idols! We may usefully refer to Psalm 115 for our most complete catalog of the impotence of idols, a catalog echoed in our poem:

> Their idols are silver and gold,
>   the work of human hands.

> They have mouths, but do not speak;
> eyes, but do not see.
> They have ears, but do not hear;
> noses, but do not smell.
> They have hands, but do not feel;
> feet, but do not walk;
> they make no sound in their throats.
> Psalm 115:4–7

The accent is on the negative: not speak, not see, not hear, not smell, not walk, not clear their throat! They cannot do anything. They cannot save; they cannot hear a prayer. They cannot care; they cannot forgive; they cannot heal.

The zinger in the psalm is verse 8:

> Those who make them are like them;
> so are all who trust in them.

Worshipers of idols become like the idols they worship, fated to be impotent and ineffective:

> What wrong did your ancestors find in me
> that they went far from me,
> and went after worthless things, and became worthless
> themselves?
> Jeremiah 2:5

The term "worthless" means "bubble"—vapor, something without substance. Those who bet their lives on idols have no staying power; they cannot endure or prevail amid the vagaries of history.

On all counts YHWH is unlike the idols. The phrase is repeated:

> None like you (Jeremiah 10:6)
> No one like you (v. 7)
> Not like these (v. 16)

Unlike the idols, YHWH is great, has a great name, is the one with which the nations must reckon (vv. 6–7). With reference to Psalm 115, YHWH can speak, see, hear, smell, feel, walk, and clear the throat! That is, YHWH is portrayed as a fully sensate agent who acts decisively in the world. In speaking this way of YHWH, we must not imagine that the poet is any more naive about YHWH than the idol worshipers are naive about their idols. The notion that YHWH has agency in the world is a stumbling block for modernity, because such an affirmation sounds superstitious and childish by the norms of Enlightenment reason. But biblical testimony does not intend to comply with Enlightenment reason. It begins at a different place. It begins in the wonder of creation and in the inexplicable emancipation of the exodus. Israel refuses to tone down its wonder at creation, and it refuses to surrender its precious memory of liberation. It does not reason to YHWH as agent; rather, it begins with YHWH as agent, so that YHWH becomes the norm and criterion for assessing truthful reality. For that reason, the Bible does not speak of YHWH's agency in modern logic, but only through the imagination of *narratives* and *doxologies of amazement* that refuse to submit to modern explanatory categories.

One can sense that the doxological verses in our poem are bursting with wonder and grasp for words and images that will give adequate voice to the inexplicable. Finally of course, such eager rhetoric will end with affirmation of YHWH as the ultimate sovereign, beyond containment by worldly power or reason:

> But the LORD is the true God;
> he is the living God and the everlasting King.
>
> v. 10

Thus God is *reliable* ("true," *'emeth*), *living* (and life-giving), and *everlasting*. YHWH must not be trifled with, even by the most powerful of nations.

Verses 12–13 offer a rich doxology to the creator God. Verse 12 gives us a triad of divine tools for creative work: by his *power*, by his *wisdom*, by his *understanding*. This is matched by three verbs of generativity (made, established, stretched out) and by three objects (earth, world, heavens). The claim is totally comprehensive of all reality. There is nothing outside the realm of YHWH's creative governance. This language is parallel to the great "whirlwind speeches" in the book of Job 38–41 that witness to the inscrutable wonder of creation that can only be the work of the creator God. Could any worshiper of an idol (wood, metal, technology, nationalism, racism) imagine an idol generating such a cosmic drama?

Verse 16 summarizes the doxological claim of the poem and then adds an important surprise. The doxological claim is that YHWH is unlike the idols—unlike in the capacity to generate and sustain a viable world. The verb "form" evokes the image of a potter shaping clay and is the same verb used in Genesis 2:7 for the formation of the human person.

In this verse YHWH is, quite remarkably, "the portion of Jacob." The term "portion" evokes land as one's special inherited property. That is, YHWH belongs peculiarly to Israel. In the last two lines of the verse, the proposition is reversed, as Israel is YHWH's "inheritance." Thus the two terms, "portion" and "inheritance," bind YHWH and Israel together in an intimate relationship that is without parallel. The final lines of the verse are a surprise in the context of the poem, which has concerned the cosmic scope of YHWH's governance. Characteristically, the Bible remains anchored in the specificities of history. For all of its lyrical affirmation about the universality of YHWH's rule, the Bible will compromise nothing of the particularity of Israel who may be, by obedience, "my treasured possession out of all the peoples" (Exodus 19:5).

Given this conclusion in specificity, we should not lose sight of the fact that at the outset the poem is a polemic against the nations and their gods (vv. 2, 7). This accent is reminiscent of YHWH's mandate to Jeremiah concerning the nations (1:10). That accent on the nations, moreover, evokes a reiteration of 10:12–16 in Jeremiah 51:15–19. The very same wording is now repeated in the context of Babylon, now a defeated nation-state that in its arrogance had contradicted the rule of YHWH (see Isaiah 47:5–11). The Babylonian gods were impotent before the rule of YHWH (see Isaiah 46:1–7), and so the God of Israel who is the God of all nations prevailed. As a consequence Israel, long-suffering at the hands of the Babylonians, had a way opened to the future beyond the terror of Babylon. The doxological reality of YHWH gives the lie to all arrogant nation-states. Nebuchadnezzar, king of Babylon, remembered the ancient glory days of Babylon in the time of Hammurabi and wanted to "make Babylon great again." But it was not possible for Babylon to be made great again, because it was grounded in an illusion of self-sufficiency, evidenced by the gods it had manufactured for itself. Both the nations and Israel finally must face the intent of the creator God; there is no viable sustainable alternative. This is the God *true, living, and everlasting*. No wonder the poet must break out in doxology.

Questions for Discussion

1. Are there idols now? Are they real?

2. How do we ourselves often prove not to be naive but still wrong?

3. Is it hard to think of God as a true agent against various idols that may be false but are nevertheless quite real?

Chapter 10

The Words of This Covenant (Jeremiah 11:8)

Yet they did not obey or incline their ear, but everyone walked in the stubbornness of an evil will. So I brought upon them all the words of this covenant, which I commanded them to do, but they did not.

Scripture Passages for Reference

Jeremiah 11
Jeremiah 15:2
Deuteronomy 5:3
Deuteronomy 28
2 Kings 23:2–3

Amid the poignant poetry of Jeremiah 2–20 there are a number of prose texts. It is likely that these prose texts have a different editorial history; they certainly speak in a somewhat different voice. The narrative of Jeremiah 11 is among the more interesting and important of these prose texts. The subject of this text is YHWH's covenant with Israel. Since the phrasing and cadences of the text are closely reminiscent of the book of Deuteronomy, it is likely that the covenant of which Jeremiah speaks is the one filtered through the tradition of Deuteronomy. The book of Deuteronomy is grounded in the covenant of Mt. Sinai (see Exodus 19–24), but it has an urgent intention to make that ancient covenant immediately contemporary: "Not with our ancestors did the LORD make this covenant, but with us, who are all of us here alive today" (Deuteronomy 5:3). Thus Jeremiah would be committed to the task of "proclamation" (11:6), whereby his own contemporaries in Jerusalem in the seventh century BCE would embrace this ancient covenant as their own.

In this text we may identify three facets of that ancient covenant. First, there are the *commandments of YHWH* (11:4). This is a reference to the Ten Commandments (Exodus 20:1–17; Deuteronomy 5:6–21; see also Jeremiah 7:9, which alludes to the commandments). Second, there is the *oath* that Israel swore to give YHWH exclusive obedience and devotion (11:5). That oath is voiced at Sinai in Exodus 24:3, 7. It is assumed that the force of the oath persists for subsequent generations, including the generation of Jeremiah. Third, "the words of this covenant" (11:8) refer to the *sanctions* that enforced the covenant—that is, blessings and curses. These sanctions are fully and extensively voiced in Deuteronomy 28. This catalog enumerates blessings for covenant obedience but offers a much more extensive list of curses to be imposed for disobedience of the Torah. This third factor means, in the tradition of Deuteronomy, that "a land flowing with milk and honey" (11:5) is conditional upon covenantal obedience to Torah commandments. That conditionality, moreover, pertains even to the generation of Jeremiah so that security in the land of promise depends upon obedience to covenant requirements.

The covenant, mediated by Deuteronomy, is old indeed. For Jeremiah and his contemporaries, however, there is a more immediate launching pad for matters of covenant. In the royal recital of the books of Kings, it is reported that King Josiah in 621 BCE renovated the temple in Jerusalem; through the renovation an old scroll was found (2 Kings 22:8). It was called the "scroll of the Torah." (It is commonly assumed by interpreters that the scroll was some form of the book of Deuteronomy.) The scroll was brought to King Josiah; when he heard it read, he was deeply moved by fear and immediately committed an act of repentance: "He tore his clothes" (22:11). The reason for his abrupt dramatic act is that he recognized that he and his people were in wholesale violation of the covenant requirements, and that they were subject to the brutal curses that came with covenantal disobedience.

Out of that dramatic moment King Josiah instituted a reform of public life in Jerusalem; he recruited his contemporaries into a new embrace of the ancient covenant:

> The king . . . read in their hearing all the words of the book of the covenant that had been found in the house of the LORD. The king stood by the pillar and made a covenant before the LORD, to follow the LORD, keeping his commandments, his decrees, and his statutes with all his heart and all his soul, to perform the words of this covenant that were written in this book. All the people joined in the covenant. (2 Kings 23:2–3)

By this public action the king intended the refounding of Israel as a covenant people under the mandates of Torah commandments. If taken seriously, this act of covenant-making (covenant renewal) was radical indeed, for the covenant was a considerable distance from the royal ideology of throne and temple. By this action of covenant-making Israel could, with high intentionality, be yet again the people of YHWH's Torah.

With this narrative background of the work of King Josiah, we may now consider the words of Jeremiah in our text. It is fair to assert that Jeremiah's narrative is in the wake of the covenant-making of King Josiah. Indeed in 11:6 the prophet reports his work of advocacy of the covenant in "the cities of Judah" and "the streets of Jerusalem." We can imagine he was an assertive, high-energy advocate for the covenant, which constituted nothing less than a reordering of the public life of Israel according to a tradition it had long neglected as much too demanding. Jeremiah's fervent advocacy of the covenant is because he is fully convinced that rule of YHWH as the defining reality of public life is the only possibility for a society that could be secure, viable, and prosperous. According to the text, he went about, seeking a reorientation of his contemporaries to this old, long-neglected tradition.

It turns out that the memory of Sinai, the dramatic initiative of King Josiah, and the advocacy of Jeremiah are all only a backdrop for our text. The point of the text turns on the "yet" at the beginning of verse 8 that does a complete reversal from the foregoing. It is the burden of Jeremiah to issue a prophetic "speech of judgment" in the wake of his advocacy for the old covenant and its commandments.

He has become convinced that the elites in Jerusalem do not intend reform and or any serious restoration of covenantal life; the covenant has in fact been rejected because the grip of royal ideology was strong and seemingly impenetrable. In his speech of judgment, the indictment is the first part of our verse. Israel did not listen! The word we translate "obey" is *shema'*, to listen. It refers to the imperative summons of YHWH to heed the commandments that are the condition of covenant. The best-known use of the term is the famous Shema of Deuteronomy 6:4, "Hear, O Israel." It is the vocation of Israel to listen to and be addressed by the Lord of the covenant. This notion of listening is the one we often use with a wayward child when we say, "You did not *listen* to me," which means, "You did not do what I told you to do." In prophetic purview, Israel characteristically does not listen, does not heed the commandments, does not keep its side of the covenant agreement. In 2 Kings 17:14–15 this indictment of "not listening" becomes the leitmotif of the entire royal enterprise in Jerusalem:

> They would *not listen* but were stubborn, as their ancestors had been, who did not believe in the LORD their God. They despised his statutes, and his covenant that he made with their ancestors, and the warnings that he gave them. They went after false idols and became false; they followed the nations that were around them, concerning whom the LORD had commanded them that they should not do as they did.

The juridical sentence of the "speech of judgment" is tersely offered in the second half of our verse: "So I brought upon them all the words of this covenant, which I commanded them to do, but they did not" (11:8). "Words of this covenant" refers to the covenant sanctions (curses) that are a part of the formal structure of the covenant. Disobedience brings disaster. According to the rhetoric of the verse, the disasters that follow disobedience are enacted through supernatural agency by the direct action of YHWH. This is a popular notion of divine judgment in the Old Testament. But we may parse the matter more carefully so that the way in which disaster follows disobedience is not so flatly supernatural. While prophetic rhetoric offers such a notion, the context of the rhetoric suggests otherwise. In other poems, Jeremiah anticipates that the disaster will take the form of "a great nation" from the north that will devastate Jerusalem (see 5:15–17; 6:22–23). In context, the phrase refers to the coming invasion of the Babylonian army dispatched by Nebuchadnezzar. Thus the prophetic juridical sentence may be understood as an insightful commentary on contemporary geopolitics over which YHWH presides.

The disasters to come, enacted through geopolitical processes, will result, according to the rhetorical inventory of the prophets, in *pestilence, war, famine, and deportation:*

> Those destined for pestilence, to pestilence,
>   and those destined for the sword, to the sword;
> those destined for famine, to famine,
>   and those destined for captivity, to captivity.
>   Jeremiah 15:2

This catalog of disasters can be understood as the inescapable outcome of geopolitical reality. Thus war can indeed produce epidemics of disease and famine and may result in deportation. This would suggest that the sovereign judgment of YHWH against a recalcitrant covenant partner is worked out in, with, and under the discernible processes of history. This is not to explain away divine judgment, but it is to see that divine judgment is not an act of magical intrusion; it is the rather inescapable working out of the consequences of self-destructive, foolish policies and conduct. This stylized catalog of disasters eventually became, in imaginative interpretation, the "four horsemen" of the apocalypse (see Revelation 6:1–8). That hyperbolic vision, however, is well beyond the sober historicity of Jeremiah. Thus Jeremiah sees that everything depends on listening, being addressed, and heeding the expectations that belong to the holy reality of God, which refuses to accommodate our favorite ideologies.

It will be a long while before Jeremiah reverses field to speak of a restored covenant. Besides this reference to broken covenant in chapter 11 and the renewed covenant in 31:31–34, we may notice two other references to covenant. In Jeremiah 22:9 Israel's abandonment of covenant is offered as a justification for the disasters that befell the city of Jerusalem. And in 14:21 in a countermove, Israel petitions YHWH not to "break your covenant with us." All of these usages speak of a fractured covenant that puts Judah at great risk.

Clearly the elite power brokers in Jerusalem had little understanding of this dimension of faith. Their public experience affirmed to them that only power, wisdom, and wealth could guarantee security and well-being. They had no time for listening.

The motif of broken covenant pertains exactly to the political economy of the United States.[1] Robert Bellah long ago showed the way in which the rise of science, the market economy, and individual capitalism had created a cultural context in which the old demands of covenant, already so well-articulated by the Puritans, have been nullified. The metrics of broken covenant in the United States include a breakdown in trust and consequently of the social fabric, the erosion of democratic institutions, and the disappearance of the common bonds between "haves" and "have-nots." The result, as Jeremiah would have well understood, is a culture of greed, fear, and violence that makes life for many of our citizens and our guests degradingly unlivable. Jeremiah articulates such a social, economic, and political emergency through the theme of covenant. He suggests that it is time for demanding, attentive listening. Amid the anguish of his own crisis, he sees that this covenantal alternative does not have a prayer, as he is prohibited from such prayer (11:14).

Questions for Discussion

1. Does disobedience still bring disaster?

2. Are good results contingent on obedience?

3. How is divine judgment not a magical intrusion but the "inescapable working out of the consequences of self-destructive, foolish policies and conduct"?

4. How does everything depend on listening?

5. Do we have a prayer (see Jeremiah 11:14)?

Chapter 11

Enticed and Overpowered! (Jeremiah 20:7)

O LORD, you have enticed me,
and I was enticed;
you have overpowered me,
and you have prevailed.
I have become a laughingstock all day long;
everyone mocks me.

Scripture Passages for Reference

Jeremiah 11:18–12:6
Jeremiah 15:10–21
Jeremiah 17:14–18
Jeremiah 18:18–23
Jeremiah 20:7–13
Job 3

Through his poetry and sermon in Jeremiah 2–20, the prophet has been intrepid, uncompromising, and unaccommodating. He has spoken truth to power. He has addressed kings in their foolish self-deception. He has castigated false prophets who have signed on with officialdom and given it legitimacy. He has exposed priests as false teachers. He has seen and voiced the truth that a regime in contradiction to the purpose of YHWH cannot stand, not even in beloved chosen Jerusalem. He has acted out his mandate from YHWH that he should be, by the will of YHWH,

> a fortified city, an iron pillar, and a bronze wall, against the whole land—against the kings of Judah, its princes, its priests, and the people of the land. (1:18)

He has done so with the assurance of YHWH's promise:

> They will fight against you; but they shall not prevail against you, for I am with you, says the LORD, to deliver you. (1:19)

Given that relentless public articulation, it would have surprised the listeners of Jeremiah, both his adversaries and those who supported him, that his public presentation was matched by an intimate hidden personal life that was filled with unresolved conflict with YHWH. Amid the public forays of Jeremiah 2–20 there is a series of "lamentations" or "confessions" that give voice to Jeremiah's restlessness with his prophetic vocation and to his disputatious interaction with the God who has summoned him (11:18–12:6; 15:10–21; 17:14–18; 18:18–23; 20:7–13). This series of poems reveals to us a prophet whose relationship with YHWH was much more conflicted and much less certain than his public utterances would have indicated.

These poems are quite stylized even while they strike us as honest and intimate. It has long been recognized that they are patterned after the familiar sequencing of psalms of lament and complaint in the book of Psalms. While there is great variation in these psalms, it is evident that there are recurring elements of speech. First, the psalms of lament and complaint are *relentlessly honest* in their address to God. They are honest about the speaker's circumstance and are often honest in their adversarial attitude toward God. Second, these psalms ask for and often receive *an answer from God* that is transformative. In the book of Psalms these honest prayers, with the exception of Psalms 39 and 88, end with a transformed voice (and transformed circumstance?) through the process of the psalms. Third, such a response from God to lament and petition permits such psalms to culminate in *an affirmative celebration*. Thus the pattern of speech is a rhetorically dramatic move from distress to affirmation or, as we might say, from alienation to reconciliation, from death to life.

At the outset of this sequence of texts concerning Jeremiah's lamentations-confessions, the prophet encounters great resistance from his listeners:

> But I was like a gentle lamb
> led to the slaughter.
> And I did not know it was against me
> that they devised schemes, saying,
> "Let us destroy the tree with its fruit,
> let us cut him off from the land of the living,
> so that his name will no longer be remembered!"
> 11:19–20

In response to such threats Jeremiah appeals to YHWH for rescue. But then he poses the large question of God's justice:

> Why does the way of the guilty prosper?
> Why do all who are treacherous thrive?
> 12:1

He sees his evil adversaries doing well. His question suggests that the fidelity of YHWH is not reliable—certainly not for him!

Ordinarily an Israelite could expect from YHWH a response of care and consolation. Here, however, God's response is hard and uncompromising. It is a call to the prophet to even harder tasks to come:

> If you have raced with foot-runners and they have wearied you,
> how will you compete with horses?
> And if in a safe land you fall down,
> how will you fare in the thickets of the Jordan?
> 12:5

This opening poem of the sequence exhibits the deep tension between Jeremiah and the God who has dispatched him. He leaves YHWH with an unanswered question: "How long?" (12:4). How long before the creator God orders the world afresh?

In the second poem the tension between YHWH and Jeremiah is intensified (15:10–21). Jeremiah reminds YHWH that he has been completely obedient and has accepted a life of loneliness in order to be faithful (15:17). In 15:18 he gives voice to his profound suffering. And then he accuses YHWH of being untrustworthy:

> Truly, you are to me like a deceitful brook,
> like waters that fail.

The image is of a wadi that carries water in the rainy season but the rest of the time is dried up. It is not a reliable source of water. YHWH is unreliable as well. YHWH has made promises to Jeremiah and is not keeping them. Again we anticipate a consoling, reassuring response. But we get instead a demanding conditional assertion from YHWH:

> If you turn back, I will take you back.
> . . . .
> If you utter what is precious . . .
> you shall serve as my mouth.
>
> 15:19

Verse 20 is an assurance to Jeremiah (as in 1:19), but it is governed by the double "if" of verse 19. This is not a full commitment to Jeremiah; it is only another summons to the prophet to be more fully committed to the work of YHWH. In his deep anguish the prophet had bid for divine assurance, but at best he gets only a grudging summons to more intense, more risky fidelity.

The third poem receives no response from YHWH (17:14–18). In the fourth poem Jeremiah voices a series of petitions to YHWH for vengeance and the settling of scores with his adversaries (18:18–23). Again there is no response!

It is likely that these five prayer-poems are arranged so that they build in intensity toward the final one in 20:7–13. The fifth poem begins at 20:7 with an intense complaint. The trouble in verses 8–10 is that Jeremiah faces an avalanche of hostility. His life is under threat. He is betrayed by his friends. He is trapped in his vocation. If he speaks "the word of the LORD," he evokes anger. But if he keeps silent he gets pain and turmoil in his body. His social situation is unbearable.

But behind his social situation is his alienation from YHWH. In that opening verse 7, he accuses God of cunning betrayal that provides the opening for the human maltreatment that follows in the poem. The opening assertion is astonishing. He repeats the word that is his primary accusation against YHWH. We translate it as "entice, entice." It can be rendered "seduce, seduce," as if Jeremiah has been tricked into his prophetic vocation. These translations, however, may be too weak. In both Hosea 2:14 (Hebrew v. 16) and Job 31:9, the term clearly has sexual connotations as a metaphor, and literal sexual connotations in Judges 14:15 and 16:5. The strongest possible rendering is "You have raped me," or more softly, "You have taken advantage of me." You have overpowered me and imposed yourself on me. And for that violent imposition, all else follows that makes his life unlivable and his vocation unbearable. The words voice the helplessness of Jeremiah in the face of his adversaries, left alone by the God who sent him and who promised to help him.

As close as we can come to this poignant sexual metaphor is the poem "Batter My Heart" by John Donne. Donne addresses the triune God ("three-person'd God") and offers a series of imperatives to God as powerful sexual invitation: at the beginning, "batter my heart," and then "divorce mee, untie, or breake that knot againe, imprison mee," and finally "ravish mee." Donne's extreme imagery is a bid for intimacy with God on God's terms. Unlike Jeremiah, Donne seeks and wants the overpowering violent attention of God, so he would be "loved in faine." Not so Jeremiah, who finds God dangerous and fickle. The sexual imagery for both the prophet and the later poet goes deeply beyond conventional theological categories to the deepest urges and hurts that can be voiced before God.

In chapter 20, as with many laments, the poem surprises us with reversal with the adversative "but" in verse 11. After his vigorous accusation, Jeremiah returns to reliance upon YHWH. In this reversal the poem reflects the standard practice of Israel's poetry. As an outcome of the reversal, the poem ends in praise (v. 13). Thus voicing the threats he experienced in verses 7–10 frees Jeremiah for a fresh embrace of faith in YHWH.

We should, however, not neglect the additional verses (14–18) that move despairingly beyond the usual pattern of lament-praise. In these verses, which are among the darkest and most forbidding in Scripture, the poet descends into unrelieved, unresolved hopelessness with a wish for nonbeing. These verses lie beyond the capacity of any interpreter, and we do not know what to make of them, and certainly not to resolve them.

It is worth noticing, however, that these same words became the entry point for the long-anguished dialogue in the book of Job (see

Job 3:1–7, 11–16). In Jeremiah the utterance of 20:14–18 is an *ending* in a thud of hopelessness. In Job, however, these same words are not an ending but the *beginning* of an engagement with God that has no parallel in Scripture; it permits a vigorous, searing theological probe. We may imagine that the argument of Job is a continuation of Jeremiah's disillusionment, because it belongs to Israel to continue the engagement even after a decisive, despairing ending. In the poem of Job, the character of Job finally voices the elemental unanswered question to God already articulated by Jeremiah in 12:2:

> Why do the wicked live on,
> reach old age, and grow mighty in power?
> Job 21:7

As the poem of Job advances, it is clear that this question about the moral coherence of God's creation is unanswerable. It was clearly unanswerable for Jeremiah, but he knew that for the sake of his sanity, his vocation, and his faith, the question had to be asked in daring honesty.

Jeremiah's deep, unflinching honesty with God, we may guess, liberated him for his hard work as a prophet. His hard work as a prophet is in contradiction to his Jerusalem contemporaries. Jeremiah's appeal to sexual imagery makes clear that he was willing and able to go to the deepest depth of his life in meeting YHWH. He did this anguished work with YHWH in a way that was mostly hidden from his contemporaries, surely in the night of his loneliness. We may imagine that after a night of such searing honesty, he was able the next day to begin again his truth-telling vocation that could arise and be sustained only through such nighttime combat.

Questions for Discussion

1. Are you comfortable with this imagery of God overpowering Jeremiah or John Donne? Why or why not?

2. Where else do you see God's overpowering presence?

3. How does candor about suffering—even the suffering of obedient saints—permit a renewed sense of vocation?

Chapter 12

On Knowing God
(Jeremiah 22:15–16)

Did not your father eat and drink
and do justice and righteousness?
Then it was well for him.
He judged the cause of the poor and needy;
then it was well.
Is not this to know me?
says the LORD.

Scripture Passages for Reference

Jeremiah 22:13–19
Deuteronomy 10:17–18
2 Kings 22–23
Luke 7:22

Jeremiah 21–24 can be roughly treated as a literary unit, perhaps by accidental arrangement. The unit is bounded at the beginning and the end by prose narratives that have Babylon in purview. In the narrative of 21:1–10 we have the first mention in the book of Babylon and its king, Nebuchadnezzar, which will dominate the remainder of the book. Babylon has been anticipated heretofore by allusions to "'a boiling pot, tilted away from the north'" (1:13), "a nation from far away" (5:15), and "a people coming from the land of the north" (6:22). This text is the first that specifies that Babylon will assault Jerusalem and bring a sword, famine, and pestilence (21:9). Because Zedekiah will be the next king, we know that the text refers to the assault by Babylon in 598 as the first deportation to Babylon (see 52:28).

The text of 21:1–10 is matched by a prose narrative concerning Babylon at the conclusion of our unit (24:1–10). In this text the king being deported in 598 is named—Jehoiachin (24:1). The text is addressed to those who have been deported in that year with the good news that God "will bring them back to this land" (24:6). Thus these two prose narratives explicate the prophetic mandate of 1:10. In 21:1–10 we have the tearing down and plucking up; in 24:1–10 we have the planting and building: "I will bring them back to this land. I will build them up, and not tear them down; I will plant them, and not pluck them up" (24:6). Thus there will be a *displacement* (into the abyss), and in due course there will be a *restoration* (out of the abyss)—the two themes of the book of Jeremiah.

It is as though the material between these two narratives is designed to show why Israel is in such big trouble and under such great threat. There are, to be sure, bids that Israel should repent; there is in particular a summons to the royal house that it should do justice for the vulnerable who are oppressed (21:12; 22:3–4). The accent of the text, however, is that it is too late, because Jerusalem has for much too long contradicted the will of YHWH.

Jeremiah has two particular targets in mind that have distorted and endangered the life of Judah. First, Jeremiah identifies the *false prophets* who have misrepresented YHWH and distorted the truth. They have signed on with misguided royal policies and have given legitimacy to them. They are the kinds of voices who declare "shalom, shalom" when there is no shalom (23:9–15, 16–17, 18–22). They "speak visions of their own minds" (23:16). They make stuff up because they have not been admitted to the "council of the LORD," a poetically construed meeting of the heavenly beings, who dispatch genuine prophets as messengers with God's truth (23:18, 22). This is the practice of civic religion that has sold out to the economic, political, exploitative ideology of the elites.

As I write this, our forty-fifth president continues to be under attack for his wholesale racism and incitement to violence. It was reported during his tenure that Black pastors met at the White House to defend the president: "I find it hard to believe" that the president is a racist. "I do not want to second guess what he says."[1] Elites can always find an accommodating prophet. Such accommodation, however, evokes from God the harshness of Babylon, says the prophet.

The second specific target of the prophet is the *failed kings* in Jerusalem who practice exploitation and disregard of Torah mandates for economic and social justice. The prophet grieves for the boy-king Jehoiachin (also called "Coniah"), because he will die without any heir (22:24–30; see 24:1). Jeremiah further grieves the devastation of the land by the invaders:

> O land, land, land,
>   hear the word of the LORD!
>   22:29

This brings us close to our specific text. Jeremiah 22:13–19 offers an oracle of judgment concerning Jehoiakim (here called "Shallum"; 22:11) with an anticipation of his degrading death. The *prophetic indictment* in verses 13–15a opens with "woe," an anticipation of death. The indictment concerns two charges. First, the king has practiced exploitative labor policy through the "injustice" of not paying his "neighbors" who do the work of the royal house (v. 13). The use of "neighbor" is likely ironic, reminding the king that even lowly workers are in fact "neighbors" who are to be treated with great regard and respect and economic fairness.

Second, the reason the king is so exploitative is that he is a "builder" who wants to enjoy luxurious residences that include upper rooms, lots of space, and windows, all extravagances beyond the means of most people. In part the king could afford these luxuries because he relied on cheap labor. Edward Baptist, in *The Half Has Never Been Told: Slavery and the Making of American Capitalism*, has shown that wealth in the United States (north as well as south) is derived from the cheap labor of slavery. Slavery in the United States is a perfect embodiment of the economic reality that wealth comes readily on the basis of cheap labor. What we know is that basis of the U.S. economy is a reiteration of this very old practice of extravagance made possible by cheap labor—and the basic dynamics of such an economy continue to recur. The king assumed such practice was legitimate, given the royal entitlement and neglect of the neighborly claims of the covenant.

The *prophetic sentence* (vv. 18–19) begins with "therefore" (i.e., because of such disregard of Torah): severe punishment for the king follows! Not only will the king die, but he will not be grieved. Nobody will remember him. Nobody will regard his death. His contemporaries will be glad he is gone. Thus the sentence includes four times, "alas," the same word that began the poetic unit in verse 13. The dead king will not receive a great royal pageant of a funeral. He will be treated like a donkey, carried away on a dead animal truck. These lines evoke a memory of Benito Mussolini, ruler of Italy, who at his death at the end of World War II had his body strung up in public humiliation in Rome.

Our interest, however, is that between the *indictment* of Jehoiakim (vv. 13–15a) and his *sentence* (vv. 18–19) our poem has inserted an astonishing contrast to the utter failure of Jehoiakim. Jehoiakim is the son of Josiah, who is named in verse 11 and is "father" in our text (see 1:3). The poem is arranged to contrast *father Josiah* and *son Jehoiakim*. We have seen how the son ended badly because of his arrogant injustice. The father, by contrast, is celebrated as a great advocate of economic justice. We know from 2 Kings 22–23 that King Josiah in 621 BCE instituted a public reform based on Deuteronomy. It was the leadership of Josiah that urgently called Israel back to covenant; the report on Josiah's action in 2 Kings 23:3 specifically alludes to Deuteronomy 6:5. In Deuteronomy we may particularly notice the characterization of YHWH, Lord of the covenant, as doer of social justice:

> For the LORD your God is God of gods and Lord of lords, the great God, mighty and awesome, who is not partial and takes no bribe, who executes justice for the orphan and the widow, and who loves the strangers, providing them food and clothing. (Deuteronomy 10:17–18)

Quite remarkably, the God of gods and Lord of lords enacts justice for the vulnerable. "No bribes" means that YHWH does not accommodate the desperately wealthy who have a capacity to bribe. Rather, this great God works economic well-being for the vulnerable— orphans, widows, and immigrants who are without protection or resources. This "high God" is deeply committed to well-being for the lowly. This remarkable linkage of "high" and "low" is asserted in

Christian tradition concerning Jesus, whom we confess as "God from God" but who attends to the poor, lame, blind, and deaf (see Luke 7:22). The characterization of YHWH in our next verse becomes an imperative to imitate this love of strangers: "You shall love the stranger, for you were strangers in the land of Egypt" (Deuteronomy 10:19). Act like YHWH! This is what covenant demands. Love vulnerable neighbors as YHWH loves vulnerable neighbors!

King Josiah clearly had this Torah requirement in purview. Thus Jeremiah can say of King Josiah in our verses, "He judged the cause of the poor and needy" (vv. 15–16). Josiah fulfilled covenant! He acted Torah! Josiah imitated the Lord of the covenant. And then he prospered. The rhetoric tacitly offers a "therefore": "He kept Torah . . . (therefore) . . . it was well with him" (v. 15). Torah obedience leads to well-being! The father is acutely contrasted to the son. The son is acutely contrasted to the father. It is impossible to imagine King Josiah acting as his son is said to have acted (vv. 13–15a). These verses go far to justify divine judgment against Jehoiakim and the coming of Babylon against Jerusalem. Thus the imperative addressed to the "house of David" and to "David" in 21:12 and 22:3–4 are summonses to the throne to do justice that would replicate Josiah and would reject the predatory royal policies and practices of Jehoiakim that had become "business as usual" in royal Jerusalem.

We come then to the extraordinary zinger in our text with the rhetorical question in the mouth of YHWH (v. 16). With reference to the economic justice practiced by King Josiah YHWH now queries, "Is not this not to know me?" The answer is "Yes!" To know YHWH truly and intimately is to enact social justice! YHWH is intimately and truly known in no other way. We notice that the statement does not say that we know YHWH and *then* do justice. Nor does it say that we do justice and *then* we get to know God. It is not one after the other, either way. Rather, doing economic justice for the vulnerable in generous, intentional ways *is* communion with God. That is because knowledge of God is not found in doctrinal proposition, in moral certitude, in disciplines of piety or spirituality, or in practices of liturgy. God shows up and discloses God's own self to us in, with, and under neighborly justice. Any other knowledge of God that comes in any other way is suspect! It is suspect even though we keep inventing strategies for knowing God apart from justice, looking for easier or more convenient or less demanding disclosure of the Holy One. This is it, for Josiah, for the royal house of David, and for the rest of us as well.

This stunning affirmation has immense practical consequences. It means that most of the quarrels in the church, most of our ideological passions, most of our strategies for proper control and governance, and most of our moral certitudes are not only irrelevant but perverse. There is no way around the truth that the actual doing of social, economic, and political justice—in neighborly practice and in neighborly policy—is how and where God meets us. King Josiah knew that. He knew it when he got the staggering impact of the scroll that shocked him to new awareness and new action (2 Kings 22:11). It is no wonder that in his response to this scroll that he fully embraced, Josiah is marked as the quintessential model of covenantal fidelity:

> Before him there was no king like him, who turned to the LORD with all his heart, with all his soul, and with all his might, according to all the law of Moses; nor did any like him arise after him. (2 Kings 23:25)

Questions for Discussion

1. In your opinion how does one best know God?

2. Where are false prophets and false kings in our world?

3. Can you identify an example of neighborly justice in our time?

4. How is communion with God seen in such acts of justice?

Chapter 13

Friends in High Places
(Jeremiah 26:24)

*But the hand of Ahikam son of Shaphan was with Jeremiah
so that he was not given over into the hands of the people to
be put to death.*

Scripture Passages for Reference

Jeremiah 7:12–15
2 Kings 22:12
Micah 3:11

As we have seen, in his temple sermon Jeremiah put the leadership
in Jerusalem on notice: because of self-destructive policies and foolish conduct Jerusalem is on course to become like ancient Shiloh,
a perpetual ruin (Jeremiah 7:12–15). This inflammatory declaration
was of course completely unacceptable and offensive to the status
quo in the city. It is not unlike the notorious declaration of Jeremiah
Wright concerning the United States: "God damn America." For his
rhetorical flight that was taken out of context, Wright eventually was
displaced in his church. His brave rhetoric was simply an echo of the
prophet, but his critics of course did not get the point. It is no great
surprise that the prophet Jeremiah's temple sermon led to his trial
with an accusation of treason.

In our present chapter 26 the sum of his sermon is reiterated, again culminating with an allusion to Shiloh (26:6). It is the religious leadership of the city, prophets and priests, who instigate charges against Jeremiah (vv. 8, 11). The crowd joins with the religious officials in wanting the death sentence for the prophet. The mob behavior of the drama is replicated in the trial of Jesus (Matthew 27:22–23; Mark 15:13–14) and in our own time in the Trumpian mantras "Lock her up" and "Send her back." It is easy enough to mobilize the crowd in mindless defense of the status quo. In the face of that aggressive action, the "officials"—that is, the civic leadership—rejected the urging of the religious leaders and acquitted Jeremiah of the charges. Thus the actual drama of the trial is quickly resolved.

Our attention, however, is on two features of the narrative that function on behalf of the accused prophet. Both of these features merit attention if we are to understand the person of Jeremiah and the book of Jeremiah in social context. First, it is reported in 26:17–19 that "elders" from a rural village intervened in the trial. Such an intervention must itself have been dramatic. The rootage of the elders in village life reminds us of the deep tension that existed between such villagers who likely lived a subsistence life and the city dwellers whose standard of living prospered on the backs of subsistence peasants. Thus there was built-in resentment between the elders and the city where they intervened. These villagers, moreover, come from a place not unlike Anathoth, the home village of Jeremiah. Thus they must have been sympathetic to him and resonated with his message that critiqued the urban establishment. Such villagers, moreover, have long memories. In this instance they remember one of their own, Micah, who had voiced prophetic utterance a century before, perhaps about 715 BCE. At that point in time there was as yet no canonical book of Micah, but only remembered utterances. Here in Jeremiah 26:18, the elders quote from Micah 3:12 in its anticipated trouble for the city. In Micah, that devastating anticipation was evoked by the distortions of the city:

> Its rulers give judgment for a bribe,
>   its priests teach for a price,
>   its prophets give oracles for money;
> yet they lean on the LORD and say,
>   "Surely the LORD is with us!"
>   Micah 3:11

This is a remarkable instance of the Bible quoting the Bible. The elders remember that Micah had threatened Jerusalem, but King Hezekiah had been a pious king and did not execute him. Instead King Hezekiah received the prophetic word and turned to the Lord in repentance. The elders cite this case as ground for acquittal of Jeremiah. The people of God are to host and take seriously the prophetic word, even when it is unwelcome and it rubs the wrong way. It is against the character of the covenant community to resist such utterance of dangerous truth. In citing Micah, we can see that long-established prophetic tradition can have a durable effect amid an attentive public.

The other quite remarkable notice in this narrative is our verse 24. It is reported that Ahikam, son of Shaphan, was supportive of Jeremiah. It turns out that Ahikam has his fingerprint all over the dramatic crisis concerning Jeremiah. In 2 Kings 22:12 he is among those dispatched by King Josiah to follow up on the scroll of Deuteronomy found in the temple. More importantly, Ahikam is the father of Gedaliah, who was appointed by the Babylonians to be governor of Judah after the last Davidic king had been terminated (39:24; 40:5, 7, 9, 11, 14, 16; 42:2, 6, 10, 16; 43:6). This was quite an important public appointment. Like most conquering forces, the Babylonians, after their victory over Jerusalem, did not rule directly. Rather, they chose a trustworthy "local" to represent their continuing interests reliably. That the Babylonians chose Gedaliah, a member of the prominent political family of Shaphan, means that the family was respected and trusted by the Babylonians. This would suggest that the family of Shaphan had pro-Babylonian sentiments well before this moment. These pro-Babylonian sentiments would have been in agreement with the advocacy of Jeremiah. The prophet had urged the king not to resist Babylon but to submit. He no doubt recognized that resistance to Babylon was suicidal for Judah. He interpreted Babylon as an agent of YHWH acting to implement YHWH's judgment against the faithless city. Thus the family of Shaphan was readily allied with Jeremiah in making an argument for a pro-Babylonian policy that refused the anti-Babylonian stance of the throne. The alliance between Jeremiah and Shaphan thus included both theological and pragmatic dimensions.

The reason for attending to this historical notice in our verse is in order that we may acknowledge that Jeremiah had powerful allies in high and influential places. Or said another way, Jeremiah was not a loner. He was rather the point person for a strong political opinion in Judah that opposed present royal leadership. Robert Wilson has termed such a prophet "peripheral," at the edge of social power.[1] But "peripheral" does not at all mean "isolated." It only connotes being outside of official leverage. Thus Jeremiah is party to a dispute over the wisest policy of action for Jerusalem in the face of encroaching Babylon. We are able to see that the work of Jeremiah is not simply as a lone "religious" voice spouting religious claims in the name of YHWH. He is part of an advocacy for a policy that wants to protect the people from foolhardy, self-destructive bravado. Such policy is under the illusion that being the chosen people, chosen city, and chosen king would grant a pass on geopolitical reality.

One other note likely pertains. The frightened, panicky king, Jehoiakim, sends a posse to arrest Jeremiah and his secretary, Baruch. The king sees them as treasonable and wants to stop them from further agitation against his regime. It turns out that Jeremiah and Baruch are able to elude the royal posse and are not arrested. In its comment on their escape from the posse, the text only says laconically, "The LORD hid them" (36:26). No explanation for their deliverance is offered. The words themselves might suggest some swoop-in supernatural rescue. Given what we know about the political reality of the moment, however, we may surmise that this terse phrase conceals the prospect that Jeremiah and Baruch were hidden and protected, not by direct divine action but by attentive allies, perhaps from the family of Shaphan. We may imagine that it was such allies that provided a safe house to keep them beyond the reach of the king. Thus we may read that YHWH hid them in 36:26 in light of 26:24: "The hand of Ahikam son of Shaphan was with Jeremiah."

I have cited *the quotation of prophetic poetry* from Micah 3:12 and *the intervention of Ahikam* to protect Jeremiah because these two notions invite a reconsideration of the work of Jeremiah and the broader work of prophetic utterance. The citation of Micah suggests that Jeremiah is deeply rooted in an ongoing tradition of prophetic truth-telling of the kind Daniel Berrigan has boldly done in our own time. Such prophetic poetry is not some odd, divine, isolated utterance. It is, simply put, poetry offered by those with great moral passion who simply must speak out. The fact that this speech strikes us as odd, divine, and inspired is because, like the ancients who resisted such speech, we have become inured to official-speak that has no capacity for truth or newness. Each new poet who does such work is no doubt informed, sustained, and empowered by those who have uttered such truth before. Such poetry, as Harold Bloom has seen, is not de novo, but is evoked under the influence of predecessors.[2]

The reference to Ahikam dissuades us from any notion of the prophet as "loner." Jeremiah was not the only one in his social context who had such insight and such passion. He was no doubt glad to rely on the powerful support of Ahikam and no doubt glad that Ahikam's son, Gedaliah, had some continuing influence. Indeed, we may say that Ahikam did the urgent work of "lay ministry" at its best. He made sure that the prophet had maintenance and support to continue his bold truth-telling. Thus Jeremiah was deeply situated, in *tradition* and in *contemporary politics*, even if his work sounded odd and treasonable to the royal establishment. That is because the royal establishment, as is often the wont of the powerful, knew nothing of social thickness, the very thickness that is indispensable for effective prophetic utterance. The king's misunderstanding of such thickness is evident in his assumption that he could dispose of the prophetic scroll with a little fire (36:23).

Questions for Discussion

1. Where do you experience divine poetry against official-speak?

2. Can you identify examples of friends in high places who have protected prophetic voices?

3. Can you imagine yourself in one of these roles?

4. What might one do to keep prophetic poetry alive today?

Chapter 14

Behind Treason . . . God?
(Jeremiah 27:5)

*It is I who by my great power and my outstretched arm have
made the earth, with the people and animals that are on the
earth, and I give it to whomever I please.*

Scripture Passages for Reference

Jeremiah 27–28
Daniel 4

We have seen in 23:9–22 Jeremiah's harsh strictures against prophets who oppose him and his witness. He dismisses them as phonies
who are not authorized by YHWH but who make up their own mes-
sages. It turns out that these "false prophets" are not simply liars who
distort reality. The fact is that they have signed on with the dominant
ideology of the Jerusalem elites and give that ideology legitimacy.
Their claim, echoing the throne and temple, is that David is the chosen king and Jerusalem is the chosen city, and no evil can befall
them because they are peculiarly loved and protected by YHWH.
Jeremiah declares that ideology to be false. He does so by appealing
to the ancient covenant of Sinai with its rigorous Torah requirements
and its weighty sanctions of blessing and curse. The issue between
Jeremiah and the "false prophets" is a life-or-death contest between
competing versions of covenantal faith.

That systemic conflict is given dramatic specificity in the narrative confrontation of Jeremiah 27–28. In the preparatory work of chapter 27, Jeremiah receives instruction from YHWH in 598 BCE, just after the first deportation to Babylon that included King Jehoiachin. Jeremiah is to wear a "yoke" in a dramatic representation of the imperial force of Babylon that will weigh heavily on Judah and on all the kingdom of the region (27:2). In this moment of street theater, Jeremiah not only anticipates Babylonian domination; he affirms that the mastery of the Babylonian king, Nebuchadnezzar, is the will of YHWH. Thus in 27:5 Jeremiah has YHWH declare, "It is I" who has given governance to Nebuchadnezzar, who is here termed YHWH's "servant" who does the will of YHWH. It is difficult to imagine a more treasonable assertion in Jerusalem than that the enemy, Nebuchadnezzar, is the agent of YHWH!

Jeremiah articulates, for the nations and for his king, Zedekiah, a counterintuitive either-or. If there is *submission* to Nebuchadnezzar, the Babylonian king will leave the people safely in the land (27:11–12). But if there is *resistance* to Babylon, there will be sword, famine, and pestilence (27:8–10). Jeremiah urges his people and his king to accept the Babylonian conquest as the will of YHWH.

With that background we may consider the remarkable confrontation in the temple between Jeremiah and his nemesis, Hananiah (chap. 28). Hananiah reiterates the assurance that Jerusalem will be safe from Babylon. He must, perforce, acknowledge the deportation of 598 that has just happened, but he insists it will end very soon, within two years (v. 3). Hananiah judges that YHWH's devotion to Jerusalem will not permit Babylon to prevail very long. We may notice that his name, Hananiah, means "YHWH is gracious." That is a summary of Jerusalem ideology. YHWH is gracious to Jerusalem, so nothing bad can happen here! Hananiah mouths an easy assurance that must have pleased the leadership in the temple, because official leadership is always offering assurance that the worst is over and things are just about to get better: "The war will end soon!" "The economy has bottomed out!" "The environment will be improved!" Very often, as here, these assurances are self-deceiving illusions.

All this time Jeremiah has been wearing a dramatic yoke to remind his listeners of the reality of Babylonian domination that is authorized by YHWH. Hananiah's response to Jeremiah's dramatic performance is to break the yoke from the neck of Jeremiah, signifying that the yoke of Babylon is momentary and not long-term (v. 10). Jeremiah responds promptly and frontally (vv. 13–16). He does not put on a new yoke, but he appeals to the image of a yoke. He answers that Hananiah has broken a wooden yoke but that the real yoke of Babylonian occupation is iron and cannot and will not be broken by the wish world of Hananiah (v. 13). Jeremiah declares that YHWH has put the iron yoke of Babylon over all the nations of the area. Babylonian control will be long-lasting and will withstand every challenge. It is, moreover, willed by YHWH so that Nebuchadnezzar can be identified as "my servant" (25:9; 27:6). It was for sure a scandal for Jeremiah to identify the great enemy of Judah as YHWH's "servant." It would not be unlike, in our present circumstance, the identification of the ayatollah in Iran as "God's servant" against our American national pride. No doubt the prophet meant it to be as scandalous as he can imagine, because he sees the self-confident ideology of Jerusalem as a dangerous and death-bringing illusion through which the leadership lives in a make-believe world of well-being. YHWH has handed governance over to Nebuchadnezzar! Indeed, in verse 14 the prophet asserts that Nebuchadnezzar is lord even of "the wild animals"—that is, of all creation.

Jeremiah adds a personal note concerning Hananiah (v. 16). He declares that Hananiah will die "within a year" because he has spoken falsely about YHWH's governance of the world. In verse 17 the narrative adds tersely, "Hananiah died." Jeremiah is vindicated. Falsehood cannot stand. The entire narrative is a vindication of the prophetic word of Jeremiah.

This narrative concerns competition between two ideological claims and visions of public reality. It is also, however, a sweeping theological statement concerning the sovereignty of YHWH. Thus in 27:5 YHWH is permitted a first-person declaration: "It is I." It is not Nebuchadnezzar; it is not Babylonian armies. The assertion leaves no doubt that YHWH is Lord and master of history. The final claim of our verse, moreover, is that YHWH is utterly free to assign governance to whomever YHWH chooses. YHWH, it turns out, is not finally committed to David or to Jerusalem or to Israel. And here the mighty sovereign God has, without giving any explanation, assigned governance to Nebuchadnezzar of Babylon. The outcome is a deep inexplicable subversion of all taken-for-granted assumptions of political power in Jerusalem.

What had happened in Jerusalem is that the sovereignty of YHWH had been, by temple liturgy and royal ideology, shrunken and confined to the chosen king, chosen city, chosen temple, and chosen people; the rule of YHWH had become coterminous with the well-being of Israel. Such reduction of YHWH's rule, however, is an illusion that cannot be sustained. Thus YHWH's glorious rule is affirmed and celebrated by the prophet at the expense of Jerusalem's self-assurance.

We may see the same drama played out in the book of Daniel, only now the shoe is on the other foot. In the narrative of Daniel 4, Nebuchadnezzar has come to great power by the will of the God of heaven. He imagines, however, that he is self-sufficient. In response to his hubris, the God of heaven will take Nebuchadnezzar down several notches: ". . . until you have learned that the Most High has sovereignty over the kingdom of mortals, and gives it to whom he will" (Daniel 4:25; reiterated in v. 32). Consequently, Nebuchadnezzar is denied his royal power and reduced to humiliation as a grass-eating animal.

As the narrative eventuates, it is reported that Nebuchadnezzar, in the insanity of his great power, had gone berserk. Now he receives his sanity back. His sanity consists in his recognition that he is accountable to the Lord of all history who has empowered him; for that reason he ends in doxology in which he submits himself to the ultimate rule of God: "Now I, Nebuchadnezzar, praise and extol and honor the King of heaven." In his sanity he receives his rule again and acknowledges the character of real power that is accountable to the God of heaven:

> for all his works are truth,
>   and his ways are justice;
> and he is able to bring low
>   those who walk in pride.
>   v. 37

Extracting an analog from these narratives to our own political context is not easy or obvious. It is easy enough, however, to see that U.S. exceptionalism, driven by white arrogance, has assumed that the future and well-being of the United States are coterminous with the will of God. And of course such a presumption has invited and legitimated greedy predation on many occasions. We might learn from this prophetic confrontation with Hananiah that every easy assumption about God's special people is highly suspect. In the end, as even Nebuchadnezzar had come to see, God's rule is one of righteousness and mercy (Daniel 4:27); God's will is for truth and justice (4:37). These markings of God's rule are not compromised for the sake of any chosen people.

Thus we sing:

> This is my Father's world.
> O, let me ne'er forget
> that though the wrong seems oft so strong,
> God is the ruler yet.[1]

We sing these hymn lines to a benign comforting melody. But the claim "God is the ruler yet" has more bite to it than that. In spite of evidence otherwise, God is the ruler yet. In spite of arrogant self-assurance, God is the ruler yet. In spite of self-deceiving overreach, God is the ruler yet. In our case, 9/11—not unlike the fall of Jerusalem to Babylon—was a disaster for the illusion of exceptionalism, a disaster completely disproportionate to the actual damage. The work of Jeremiah, in the face of Hananiah, is to help his people come to terms with the reality that "God is the ruler yet." Over all of our little systems of meaning and power, there is this dread-filled assertion, "It is I."

Questions for Discussion

1. Where do you see signs that "God is the ruler yet"?

2. Are you comfortable with the notion of God at work behind the destruction of certain ideologies of prestige and power? Why or why not?

3. How does Jeremiah help with this idea?

4. If you can imagine being there for this prophetic confrontation, would you likely be on Hananiah's or Jeremiah's side of things? Why?

Chapter 15

Peace in Exile? Peace for Babylon? (Jeremiah 29:7)

But seek the welfare of the city where I have sent you into exile, and pray to the LORD on its behalf, for in its welfare you will find your welfare.

Scripture Passages for Reference

Jeremiah 1:10
Jeremiah 29:1–4
Deuteronomy 4:29
Deuteronomy 6:5
Isaiah 55:8–9
Isaiah 56:8

Jeremiah's letter to the exiles dates to 598 BCE, just after the first deportation to Babylon (29:1; see also 52:28; 2 Kings 24:8–12). From that point on in the book of Jeremiah (and more broadly in Jewish history) there were two populations of Israelites: the people who had *remained in the land*, and the ones *deported*, a company that included the king and the royal entourage and various artisans. As is evident in our chapter and in the book of Jeremiah more generally, there was a continuing unresolved tension between those two populations. The tension concerned the question of who had acted faithfully and who would be the authentic carrier of Judaism into the future. It is the question that long divided the community; it is, moreover, the question that often arises in a social conflict, not least in church quarrels (e.g., "Who are the authentic carriers of Presbyterianism?"). It arises now among us amid rising racist ideology: "Who are the real Americans?" In the ongoing work of tradition, the deportees seized the initiative and became commonly recognized as the authentic carriers of Judaism. We can see both this conflict and this resolution being played out a century later with Ezra and Nehemiah.

Jeremiah weighs in on that dispute by his letter to the deported community, thus adding his voice to their claim of legitimacy. Perhaps the most important and interesting matter is that Jeremiah writes the letter at all, a highly unusual gesture. Jeremiah's sympathy had long been pro-Babylonian. He had urged his listeners to submit to Babylon, and now he endorses those who have submitted and are deported. (The alternative to such submission, in his judgment, was far worse.) His letter serves to acknowledge the deported community as a legitimate element in the community of Jews to whom no fault can be attributed. It has turned out to be the case historically that this community in exile claimed a pedigree as faithful Jews who would come to exercise important leadership in defining and performing the history of Judaism. The capacity of this community of deportees to persevere brings with it the truth-telling recognition that Jews can be legitimately Jews outside of the land of promise. Thus this community is the beginning of a Jewish diaspora, a worldwide scattering of Jews who have long since exercised leadership in defining Judaism. In our lifetime, the founding of the state of Israel has of course added complexity to the question. But even so, there is no doubt that authentic Judaism is practiced in many places other than in the land of promise. The interaction of Jews in exile and Jews in the homeland is filled with tension. Interaction between the two, nonetheless, continued to be important; neither party can be dismissed from the work of faithful Judaism.

In the first paragraph of this letter (vv. 4–9) we may take note of three accents. First, Jeremiah urges the deportees to settle in and make a life in Babylon, because there will be no ready homecoming for them. Exiles are in this abyss of displacement for the long term. Jeremiah's imperatives in verse 5, build and plant, pertain to the particularity of having settled homes and fruitful gardens that last into the next season. The two terms also echo YHWH's verbs of restoration from 1:10, so that the deportees are to replicate the restorative capacity of YHWH, only they are to do that restorative work in Babylon. Their long-term habitation of this new "homeland" (Babylon!) indicates extendedness into the next generations. The deportees are not to think of their Babylonian context as a way station, but as a home for building, planting, multiplying, and investing.

Second, verse 7 is a remarkable imperative to the deportees. They are to seek for—that is, work for—the well-being of the city of Babylon. They are not to regard Babylon with hostility, but as an environment to which they may make a positive contribution. The term we render "welfare" is *shalom*. We have seen how *shalom* is a tag word related particularly to Jeru-*salem* and to the family of *Solomon*. The term is, moreover, the mantra of the "false prophets" who continued in Jerusalem to proclaim *shalom* when in fact there was none. Thus it is a bold move by Jeremiah to declare that *shalom* can be found elsewhere; the deportees are to be committed to *shalom* for the city so long feared. The prophet knew that deported Jews can never have a "separate peace," a season of private well-being, if the host city is not a venue for *shalom*. This is a stunning declaration that Jews are to come to terms with the reality of Babylon, to contribute to its prosperity, and to benefit from that common prosperity. The deported Jews are urged to find ways to accommodate the real world in which they find themselves.

Third, it is evident in verses 8–9 that Jeremiah was still opposed by the advocates of the opinion of Hananiah, who continued to anticipate that there would be an early return home, a verdict that Jeremiah mightily resisted. It can be concluded that this remarkable pastoral letter went far to reconfigure what it meant to be a Jew, defining the new work of Jews that had not been necessary as long as Jews lived in their own land. Now Jews had to reckon with a very different environment. It is of course not different for Christians who also need to come to terms with a variety of cultural social environments, some of which are hostile to gospel faith. It can easily be argued that in the world of the West, Christians have been much too accommodating to alien cultural claims so that the deep claims of faith have largely evaporated into the cultural scene. Thus for Christians as for Jews, the matter of *accommodation and/or distinctiveness* remains a demanding issue that requires endless attentiveness and intentionality.

It is likely that the letter of Jeremiah does not itself extend beyond verse 9. The continuing tradition of Jeremiah, however, has added important material beyond the scope of his letter. Verses 10–14 constitute some of the most sweeping and most eloquent of Jeremianic promises. We may note in these verses three phrases that have readily become classic in exilic hope. First, YHWH has a "plan" for Jerusalem that will be a future of *shalom*. The term "plan" is tricky; it likely does not mean "blueprint" but rather an intention over which YHWH will watch to bring to fruition (see Isaiah 55:8–9). The God of Israel is the God of hope who creates new futures, who makes a way out of no way. God's intention for Israel is finally not punishment, judgment, or suffering displacement, but *shalom*. It is impossible to overstate the force of the coming future for Jerusalem and for biblical faith in which Christians share. Thus Jesus' proclamation of the coming "kingdom of God" is derived from this mighty prophetic hope. That kingdom of God, of course, is not otherworldly; it is a vision of an earthly regime come to full *shalom*. Second, God is not remote from or detached from or hidden from the exilic community. If one thought YHWH could be found only in the Jerusalem temple, the deportees would have no access. To the contrary, this text insists that God is "findable" by deportees where they are, if they have diligence in faith. The rhetoric of "all your heart" is of course reminiscent of the primal mandate of Deuteronomy 6:5: "You shall love the LORD your God with all your heart. . . ." This assurance is paralleled in the mouth of Moses in Deuteronomy 4:29. Moses has just announced the "scattering" of Israel. And then he says promptly this: "*From there* you will seek the LORD your God, and you will find him if you search after him with all your heart and soul." "From there" means "from Babylon." The phrase "all your heart" is intensified with "and soul [*nephesh*]." Thus God will be known as a future-creating agent among deported Jews who are serious about their trust in YHWH.

Third, and most important, the phrase "restore your fortunes" becomes a point of rally for the exiles (see Jeremiah 30:3, 18; 31:23; 32:45; 33:7, 11, 26). The phrase means that YHWH will reverse course. The "scattered" Jews will be "gathered":

"He who *scattered* Israel will *gather* him,
    and will keep him as a shepherd a flock."
                                Jeremiah 31:10

Thus says the Lord GOD,
    who *gathers* the outcasts of Israel,
I will *gather* others to them
    besides those already *gathered.*
                                Isaiah 56:8

YHWH is *gatherer* of *scattered* Jews. There will be homecoming. Even though there is to be planting, building, multiplying, and investing in Babylon long term, that long term is not to perpetuity. For this part of the book of Jeremiah, in chapters 30–33, accent is on the wonder of homecoming. The poetry in these chapters is lyrical in its expectation. Amid that poetry, the narrative of chapter 32 is more specific and grounded:

> For thus says the LORD of hosts, the God of Israel: Houses and fields and vineyards shall again be bought in this land. . . . Yet you, O Lord GOD, have said to me, "Buy the field for money and get witnesses"—though the city has been given into the hand of the Chaldeans. . . . I will make an everlasting covenant with them, never to draw back from doing good to them; and I will put the fear of me in their hearts, so that they may not turn from me. I will rejoice in doing good to them, and I will plant them in this land in faithfulness, with all my heart and all my soul. (32:15, 25, 40–41)

Thus the tradition of Jeremiah makes two points on the future of Israel without compromising either of them. On the one hand, exile is long term. On the other hand, exile is not to perpetuity. YHWH is *Lord of the exile* who wills YHWH's people to be in a strange land. YHWH is the *Lord of homecoming* and will bring it to fruition. Everything depends, in this perspective, on the truth that YHWH is Lord of history. From that, it follows that the people of YHWH must attend to the will of YHWH, both *shalom* for Babylon and *shalom* upon returning home. Both assignments require intentionality and courage.

The outcome of chapter 29 makes clear that the earlier dispute with Hananiah persisted. Jeremiah's present opponent, Shemaiah, accurately quotes Jeremiah in 29:28; however, he regards that statement of Jeremiah as false, uttered by a "madman" (*meshuga'*, v. 26). It turns out that the daring, unconventional assertion of Jeremiah is not that of a madman. It is rather the word of a truth-teller who does not doubt the power and good faith of YHWH and who does not echo the popular self-deceived cant of Jerusalem.

Questions for Discussion

1. How best does one negotiate the problem of accommodation versus distinctiveness?

2. Are people living in exile now? Where and how?

3. How do you see God as the Lord of both exile and homecoming?

4. What would it look like to seek peace (*shalom*) for our enemies while we are in exile?

Chapter 16

Reversing Field for Zion's Sake (Jeremiah 30:17)

For I will restore health to you,
and your wounds I will heal,
                    says the LORD,
because they have called you an outcast:
"It is Zion, no one cares for her!"

Scripture Passages for Reference

Jeremiah 29:11–14
Jeremiah 30:12–17
Jeremiah 31:3
Exodus 15:26
Numbers 14:16
Ezekiel 36:24–28

Clustered together in Jeremiah 30–33 are a series of divine promises through which YHWH avows to bring deported Israel back to the land of promise and to Jerusalem. In 30:2 this collection of promises is termed a "book" ("write for yourself") so that interpreters refer to these chapters as "the Book of Comfort," whereby YHWH comforts Israel in its loss and displacement by assurances of homecoming. It is likely that this scroll existed independently and was incorporated into the larger scroll of Jeremiah at this point in order to explicate the grand promises of YHWH in 29:11–14. Within this collection of divine promises, I have chosen to comment on 30:17, which is the conclusion of the shorter poem of 30:12–17. I take this promissory poem to be representative of the entire collection of promises, all of which feature YHWH articulating a new resolve on behalf of the exiles.

In 30:17 YHWH declares, "I will restore health. . . . I will heal." The punishment and displacement of Israel are here regarded according to the image of wound or sickness. We can see the same imagery, filled with pathos, voiced in 8:21 concerning the "hurt" of Israel:

> For the hurt of my poor people I am hurt,
> I mourn, and dismay has taken hold of me.

We have known that YHWH is a healer since YHWH's self-announcement in Exodus 15:26: "'I will not bring upon you any of the diseases that I brought on the Egyptians; for I am the LORD who heals you.'" In that instance YHWH resolves to overcome the "diseases of Egypt." While interpreters have been vexed about a medical identification of those diseases, when we stay inside the text it seems more likely that the "diseases of Egypt" consist of injustice, oppression, greed, and violence. The exodus amounts to a healing of enslaved Israel from all of these pathologies. When we move from the book of Exodus to the book of Jeremiah, we are aware that Jerusalem was beset by the same diseases as was old Egypt—injustice, oppression, greed, and violence—recurring subjects of prophetic indictments of Judah. Now YHWH resolves to "heal" Israel from those maladies, suggesting that restored Israel will be able to live disease-free and so able to practice social, economic, and political justice that it is not propelled by greed or fear.

YHWH's resolve to "heal" Israel is all the more dazzling because in this same poem, in earlier verses, YHWH had declared that Israel is beyond healing:

> Your hurt is incurable,
>   your wound is grievous.
> There is no one to uphold your cause,
>   no medicine for your wound,
>   no healing for you.

. . . .
Your pain is incurable.
Jeremiah 30:12–13, 15

The wonder of the structure of the poem is that it moves from "incurable" (vv. 12, 15) to "restore health" and "heal" (v. 17). When we trace the rhetoric of the poem, we can see that there is a dramatic reversal between verses 15 and 16. Verse 15 still affirms that Israel is beyond healing. Verse 16 is introduced by "therefore," a tag word that in the prophets characteristically introduces a prophetic sentence of judgment. Thus after verse 15 we expect the "therefore" of verse 16 to be followed by more divine threat. But it is not! Instead, it is followed by a reversal in verse 16 so that YHWH will trash all those who devour and plunder Israel—that is, Babylon. YHWH's anger is turned from Israel to Babylon. And after that resolve of threat in verse 16 against the enemies of Israel, verse 17 declares healing for Israel.

The interesting question of verses 16–17 is what happened in the poem to cause the reversal? Or if we approach the question with theological "realism," we may ask what happened to YHWH in the midst of the poem so that YHWH reverses field from "incurable" to "heal." The poetry does not answer the question. We may nonetheless conclude that according to poetic imagination YHWH has a change of heart or a surge of awareness that causes a new resolve on the part of YHWH. Of course all of this is only the imagination of the poet, but that is all we have to go on. We will, for now, regard this poetry as revelatory of the internal life of YHWH to which the poet imagines access. According to that imaginative act, YHWH initiates a fresh positive intent as divine anger toward Israel seems to have been spent and exhausted.

Perhaps we are given a clue to the nature of this divine change of heart in the last line of verse 17. The introductory preposition of the last line is translated "because." If we take that translation (a choice, not a requirement), the last line gives a reason why YHWH has reversed field. The reason is that YHWH had heard other nations mocking Israel in exile and concluding that Israel was hopeless in exile ("driven out"), left abandoned, for whom no one cares. There was ample evidence for other peoples to conclude that God had failed and abandoned the people of Israel; that is how it appeared! In the hardball world of ancient political theology, Israel's adversaries would be quick to draw such a conclusion. There is a precedent for that when Moses compels YHWH to save desperate Israel in the wilderness so that the nations would not draw a wrong conclusion about YHWH's capacity to save. Moses did not want the inhabitants of the land to say, "It is because the LORD was not able to bring this people into the land he swore to give them that he has slaughtered them in the wilderness" (Numbers 14:16).

The nations will conclude that YHWH lacked power. In the case of Moses, that was sufficient motivation for YHWH to save Israel. Now centuries later in Jeremiah, the same transaction is reperformed. The nations are mocking Israel in exile and by implication are judging YHWH to be impotent or unreliable. The "failure" of exile leads to the mocking of Israel and the mocking of YHWH, both of which YHWH finds unacceptable. In response to that mocking, YHWH reverses field and readily becomes Israel's healer and restorer. Contrary to the judgment of the nations voiced in verse 17, there is indeed someone who cares decisively for Israel in exile!

It is for that reason that YHWH reverses field and comes to the rescue of Israel that had just been declared "incurable." In that moment of noticing, YHWH comes to a new awareness of how much is at stake for both Israel and for YHWH amid the pathos of deportation. In that moment, moreover, YHWH makes a new resolve and moves from "pluck up and tear down" to begin to "build and plant" Israel in a new epoch of covenantal life.

We may imagine that YHWH comes to new awareness in this moment of poetic disclosure in two respects. First, YHWH becomes freshly aware of YHWH's own reputation among the nations and among the gods of the nations. It turns out that the deportation of Israel seemed to expose YHWH as either faithless or powerless. YHWH wants to correct that false impression. But second, YHWH becomes newly aware of *YHWH's passionate love for and commitment to Israel* that moves beyond transactional measurements. Thus YHWH here moves beyond transactional modes of relationship to self-giving, self-investing generosity. It is this deeper acknowledgment of love for Israel to which Jeremiah gives voice in 31:3:

> I have loved you with an everlasting love;
>   therefore I have continued my faithfulness to you.

YHWH had sought to dispose of fickle Israel and did "speak against him" (31:20). Having done so, however, YHWH discovers that YHWH cannot so readily dispose of "my dear son," "the child I delight in." For that reason, as many parents of wayward children discover, a more demanding reach of generous love is evoked and performed. It is this new awareness of the depth of love for Israel that evokes the turn in the poem.

We can see a different rendering of the same interaction in Ezekiel, a contemporary of Jeremiah. In Ezekiel's witness, YHWH is about to act to restore exiled Israel:

> I will take you from the nations, and gather you from all the countries, and bring you into your own land. . . . A new heart I will give you, and a new spirit I will put within you; and l will remove from your body the heart of stone and give you a heart of flesh. . . . Then you shall live in the land that I gave to your ancestors; and you shall be my people, and I will be your God. (Ezekiel 36:24, 26–28)

In Ezekiel the divine motivation for rescue is not love for Israel but God's own reputation:

> It is not for your sake, O house of Israel, that I am about to act, but for the sake of my holy name, which you have profaned among the nations to which you came. . . . It is not for your sake that I will act, says the LORD. (vv. 22, 32)

YHWH will save Israel, but the motivation is to protect divine honor and reputation. Between Jeremiah and Ezekiel there is the tension between *love for Israel* and *self-regard for YHWH*. But they yield the same good outcome. YHWH will save Israel, and all the nations will see that the restoration of Israel is an act of YHWH, who remains a powerful faithful covenant partner for Israel.

The divine reversal attested in the poem is the divine reversal that governs Israel's history of exile and homecoming. It is this divine reversal that dominates the book of Jeremiah. In our reflection on the poem, it will be crucial to recognize that the way the poet articulates YHWH is quite unlike our usual theological abstractions. The only compelling way the poet can bear witness to the wonder of YHWH that makes sense out of Israel's lived experience is by way of a poetic rendering of the internal life of YHWH. This is, so the poet attests, a God who has a deep internal life that is capable of fresh, new generative initiative. It is that fresh, new generative initiative that turns the poem to healing. It is indeed that initiative that turns the life of Israel to homecoming.

Questions for Discussion

1. What do you think about the notion of God's "internal life"?

2. Where else do you see God reversing fields?

3. Can you think of other examples of God's compassion and self-regard? What sense do you make of those categories?

4. What do you think caused the pivot in Jeremiah 30:15–16?

Chapter 17

The New Covenant
(Jeremiah 31:31–32)

The days are surely coming, says the LORD, when I will make a new covenant with the house of Israel and the house of Judah. It will not be like the covenant that I made with their ancestors when I took them by the hand to bring them out of the land of Egypt—a covenant that they broke, though I was their husband, says the LORD.

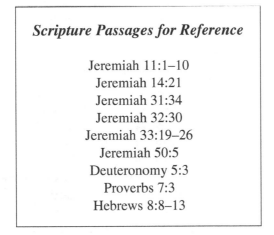

Scripture Passages for Reference

Jeremiah 11:1–10
Jeremiah 14:21
Jeremiah 31:34
Jeremiah 32:30
Jeremiah 33:19–26
Jeremiah 50:5
Deuteronomy 5:3
Proverbs 7:3
Hebrews 8:8–13

In the midst of the many promises of YHWH in the Book of Comfort (Jeremiah 30–31) and more broadly in chapters 30–33, this text on "new covenant" is the best known and arguably the most important. Jeremiah lives in the orbit of the tradition of Deuteronomy and its covenant (see Deuteronomy 5:3). Thus the covenant he has in purview is that of Mt. Sinai, to which Deuteronomy refers. In Jeremiah 11:1–10, as we have seen, the premise of the book of Jeremiah is that Israel has broken covenant and brought upon itself the harsh sanctions of that covenant. In 14:21, moreover, we have a pathos-filled petition from Israel that YHWH should honor and not break covenant:

> Do not spurn us, for your name's sake;
>> do not dishonor your glorious throne;
>> remember and do not break your covenant with us.

YHWH should keep covenant with Israel for the sake of YHWH's reputation! Of course it is the assumption of the book of Jeremiah that it is Israel, not YHWH, who has broken covenant. In Isaiah 54:7–8, the later prophet has YHWH concede that for an instant YHWH did indeed break covenant with Israel, the "instant" being the exile. That admission, however, is beyond the horizon of Jeremiah.

With the premise that Israel has broken covenant, we are hardly prepared for the astonishing declaration in 31:31–32 that YHWH, without explanation and for no reason beyond YHWH's inclination, is now about to "make a new covenant" with Israel. This covenant is in the wake of the broken Sinai covenant and is to be *unlike* the covenant of Sinai. Thus the book of Jeremiah arranges the drama of covenant as *old covenant—broken covenant—new covenant* in a way that matches the history of Israel as *the time of the kings—the time of exile—the time to come for Judaism*. This new covenant is imposed by YHWH as a *unilateral* act; it does not even require Israel's oath of allegiance, as did Sinai (see Exodus 24:3, 7). It is as though the ancient *bilateral* covenant has failed; now YHWH takes matters into YHWH's hand and acts decisively for Israel. From that remarkable act of newness, the Jeremiah tradition goes on to reflect on "the everlasting covenant" made by YHWH that will not be broken:

> I will make an *everlasting covenant* with them, never to draw back from doing good to them. (32:40)

> They shall come and join themselves to the LORD by an *everlasting covenant* that will never be forgotten. (50:5)

Indeed, in 33:19–26 the covenant YHWH makes is said to be as sure as the structure of creation established by the creator. In this text the abiding covenant is specifically with the house of David, so that the tradition, even in Jeremiah, has shifted its energy from *the bilateral covenant of Sinai to the unilateral covenant with David* (see Psalm 89:8). Thus the book of Jeremiah is moving into new interpretive and anticipatory territory that is beyond the scope of the old tradition of Deuteronomy. That interpretive, anticipatory reach in the book of Jeremiah is the ground of hope for Israel in the midst of the demise of Jerusalem and the deportation.

But while we must ponder the wonder of the new covenant, we must notice that in 31:33 there is still the mention of YHWH's Torah (that we Christians mistakenly translate as "law"). Thus for all the accent on newness, we are bound to notice that the new covenant is indeed quite *like* the old covenant in which Israel is bound to keep Torah. Thus we must entertain the recognition that the new covenant YHWH will make is in fact a remaking of the Sinai covenant. Thus the new covenant is both *like* and *unlike* the old covenant, so that this tradition affirms both *discontinuity from* and *continuity with* the old practice of covenanting.

The covenant is unlike the old in that it will not be a relationship that is quarrelsome, contested, and adversarial. There will be no resistance to the old commandments but rather glad willingness to obey. It will be like the old covenant in which there are indeed Torah requirements that provide the expectations and structure for the relationship. Thus our text marvelously imagines a new faithfulness whereby recalcitrant Israel is now responsive Israel. The capacity for ready obedience is that Israel will have internalized the commands of Torah as its very own. The notion of Torah written on the heart seems to be appropriated from the wisdom tradition, wherein parental instruction has so inculcated family teaching that it is engraved as the moral compass of the young (see Proverbs 7:3). Now engraved in the heart of Israel are not family teachings but the teaching (Torah) of the Lord of the covenant. YHWH will, moreover, give Israel a "new heart"—that is, a new willingness to be in sync with the Lord of the covenant. The Torah requirements will be so embraced and accepted that there will be no need for Torah instruction in the community. Everyone will know; everyone will gladly embrace and obey as one's willing way to live. Such embrace and obedience will be as natural as breathing.

We may rightly ask, How will that be? How could such a recalcitrant people come to such a new willingness? The answer, given in verse 34, is the radical act of forgiveness. That act of forgiveness requires a new wave of passion from YHWH who had been offended by Israel. Such forgiveness is not pro forma or a liturgical act or an act of surface piety. This is a deep act of reconciliation made possible by YHWH's reach into YHWH's own passion for the relationship. It is that passion of YHWH that moves beyond all old score-keeping so that nothing of that sorry history of alienation can ever be remembered. This is an act of unilateral fidelity on the part of YHWH toward Israel, who merits no such fidelity. That is the single basis for renewal and hope for Israel.

As Christian readers, we are bound to consider the quotation of this text of new covenant in Hebrews 8:8–13, which is the longest Old Testament quotation in the New Testament. The promissory text of Jeremiah is quoted in full detail, but then it is oddly and summarily dismissed. The writer says of the covenant of Jeremiah: "In speaking of 'a new covenant,' he has made the first one obsolete. And what is obsolete and growing old will soon disappear" (Hebrews 8:13). There is no way around recognition that this text gives voice to Christian "supersessionism," the claim that Christian faith has superseded and displaced the claims of the Old Testament and consequently the claims of Judaism. That verdict is voiced in eagerness to affirm that in Jesus God has done something radically new that is discontinuous from the Old Testament. The writer of Hebrews goes on to contrast "old" worship with the worship of Christ as the "great high priest."

Supersessionism has permeated much of the Christian tradition in an eagerness to assert the newness God has wrought in Jesus. This claim made in the New Testament text and well beyond has been possible because early Christians (and the subsequent church) much too often viewed the faith of Israel in the Old Testament as over and done with. It did not reckon at all with the continuing vibrant, faithful Judaism that came to be an ongoing movement of seriously practiced faith. Thus Judaism has lived parallel to the Christian movement; the two traditions have held to many of the same views and have affirmed many of the same ethical passions in a shared witness to the same God.

Much careful work is being done to correct this mistaken supersessionism that has caricatured Judaism and that has distorted Christian faith as well. From the Christian side we may especially take note that the Vatican II document *Nostra aetate* firmly rejected supersessionism and made room for the continuing presence of Jews in the company of faith. That groundbreaking document has more recently been reconfirmed in a statement of the Pontifical Commission on Religious Relations in 1998 entitled "The Gifts and the Calling of God Are Irrevocable." The term "irrevocable" refers specifically to the durable claims of Judaism that attests Jews as God's people. The statement is the church's (albeit belated) recognition of Judaism as a continuing faithful carrier of and witness to biblical faith in a peculiar companionship with Christian faith. Parallel acknowledgments have been made by many other Christian church traditions as well.

From the side of Judaism, the document *Dabru Emet* (issued in 2000 and signed by 220 rabbis and Jewish scholars) has as its subtitle "A Jewish Statement on Christians and Christianity." The document affirms, against the centuries-long alienation of Jews and Christians with the long history of Christian supersessionism, that Jews and Christians have a common heritage and common witness for justice and peace in witness to the same God. In a word, the document anticipates that the long season of hostility may for good reason be over. It is now time for a new era of reconciliation and mutual regard for the legitimacy of the claims of the other.

The movement away from supersessionism (that is voiced by the use of our Jeremiah text in Hebrews 8) is of course welcome. That movement in a new companionship requires continuing attentiveness, honesty, and hard work. We Christians have so much to unlearn and undo. It is the case that for both Jews and Christians, God is always doing a new thing. In the context of Jeremiah, God's "new thing" was a restoration of covenant and restoration of the people in the land. In the New Testament, God's new thing was the good news embodied by Jesus. In our context, the new thing that God is doing is creating a world in which the "other" (the ones unlike "us," the conventional power people in the West: variously poor people, people of color, Muslims, immigrants, etc.) is welcomed into the expansive community of God's goodness. In that regard, God's covenant is always being renewed and resituated. We may wonder how it is possible to receive the gift of a new heart that embraces radical obedience to Torah commandments. It begins with God's inexplicable forgiveness that is God's hallmark action in the face of Jewish and Christian shared recalcitrance. In Jeremiah 31:35–37, Jeremiah asserts that the covenant with Israel is as sure as the structure of creation. It is no wonder that Christians as well as Jews receive the new covenant as God's willing unilateral act that permits common movement beyond old caricatures of the other into the bottomless generosity of God's goodness.

Questions for Discussion

1. How is the "new" covenant like and unlike, continuous and discontinuous, with the "old" covenant?

2. How is it that God is always doing a new thing?

3. Can you think of other examples of supersessionism? Can you think of strategies to resist them?

4. Does it help to remember that the first attestation of the "new" covenant (testament) is in the Old Testament (covenant)?

Chapter 18

The Restoration of Lost Land
(Jeremiah 32:15)

Thus says the LORD of hosts, the God of Israel: Houses and fields and vineyards shall again be bought in this land.

Scripture Passages for Reference

Jeremiah 32
Leviticus 25:25–28
2 Chronicles 36:22–23

Amid the wondrous promises of restoration for the deportees in Jeremiah 30–33, chapter 32 offers a narrative of hope. With the coming of the Babylonian army, land lost its value as the coming of the army was surely unsettling for the agricultural economy. The land of Israel was taken over and occupied by the Babylonian army, so that many of its erstwhile inhabitants were displaced. In the face of that displacement, Jeremiah faces responsibility to keep the family farm in Anathoth in the family while real estate values have collapsed. He is instructed by YHWH and then by his cousin Hanamel to take responsibility for the family property (vv. 6–8). It is the urging of his cousin that convinces Jeremiah that this is the intent of YHWH for him.

The prophet promptly acts on this instruction; we are provided technical details concerning the proper procedure for the transfer of property that is fully recorded (vv. 9–12). Jeremiah acts to make

103

sure that the deed is secure (vv. 13–14). And then, quite remarkably, at the behest of YHWH, Jeremiah makes a huge leap from this mundane act of transfer to an immense anticipation. Beyond present circumstance that holds no good prospect for the value of land, Jeremiah utters an anticipation for the land and in the land: "Houses and fields and vineyards shall again be bought in this land" (v. 15). The term "bought" makes clear he has in mind economic realities. This promise is uttered while the land is decimated and unproductive due to war damage. "Houses and fields and vineyards" constitute the landscape of rural or village life. Thus this anticipation of renewed agricultural life is not broad or generic; it is rather quite specific in its vision of restoration after the Babylonian destruction and occupation. This promise is a case in point of the great leap of the book of Jeremiah from the long recital of "pluck up and tear down"—the abyss of exile—to the hope of "plant and build"—the (slow) return from the abyss. "Plant" concerns fields and vineyards. "Build" concerns houses and barns. Both verbs are required for the renewal of agricultural life. The book of Jeremiah, like the people of Israel, lives through great land loss. And like Israel, the book of Jeremiah faces into restoration of the land. Indeed, the Hebrew Bible concludes with an astonishing permit to reclaim the land of promise:

> "Thus says King Cyrus of Persia: The LORD, the God of heaven, has given me all the kingdoms of the earth, and he has charged me to build him a house at Jerusalem, which is in Judah. Whoever is among you of all his people, may the LORD his God be with him! Let him go up." (2 Chronicles 36:23)

The dramatic intent of Jeremiah 32:15 is to make a compelling connection between the *specific land transaction in the village of Anathoth* and the *grand sweep of the imperial edict* of restoration. In both the specificity of Anathoth and in the imperial decree of Cyrus, it is clear that the newness YHWH will enact is this-worldly in its focus on secure living space for the people of God, the great driving hope of Israel's faith.

That great promise in verse 15 is reiterated in this extended narrative chapter:

> Yet you, O Lord GOD, have said to me, "Buy the field for money
> and get witnesses"—though the city has been given into the hands
> of the Chaldeans. (v. 25)

This verse acknowledges that the mandate is counterintuitive. The word "though" looks Babylon (Chaldea) full in the face and hopes in defiance of imperial reality. At the end of the chapter, we get one more reiteration of the promise, this time grandly sweeping:

> Fields shall be bought for money, and deeds shall be signed and
> sealed and witnessed, in the land of Benjamin, in the places around
> Jerusalem, and in the cities of Judah, of the hill country, of the
> Shephelah, and of the Negeb; for I will restore their fortunes, says
> the LORD. (v. 44)

Here we have the tag phrase "restore their fortunes." YHWH moves beyond the quid pro quo reasoning of the Sinai covenant to make unilateral promises. It is this unilateral act of YHWH that funds biblical hope and that makes a way out of no way. We may notice that in Hebrews 11, the great chapter of hope in the New Testament, faith is the readiness to seek after a "better country" (Hebrews 11:16). Thus for both Jewish and Christian faith, it is the promise of a good future from God that propels present life. Jeremiah is an urgent voice for just such a future.

It is clear that the land promise of verses 15, 25, and 44, in present circumstance, is impossible. It could not happen! Yet this is the governing prospect of Jeremiah and of the Bible. We can see that the tradition struggled with the impossible promise that became the ground for the future against all odds. In the extended prayer of 32:16–25, Jeremiah affirms in doxological language,

> It is you who made the heavens and the earth by your great power
> and by your outstretched arm! Nothing is *too hard* for you. (v. 17)

In the responding oracle of 32:26–44 YHWH asks a rhetorical question:

> I am the LORD, the God of all flesh; is anything *too hard* for me?
> (v. 27)

The answer to this question is No! In these two verses, the phrase "too hard" can be rendered "impossible." It is affirmed by Jeremiah and then by YHWH that YHWH can and will do what the world judges to be impossible. And because the world, in its socioeconomic anxiety, is propelled by hunger for land, we may consider how the "impossible possibility" of land restoration continues to be a question among us.

We have ample evidence of the way in which land hunger has led to all kinds of violence that displaces. It is easy enough to identify violent land seizures that deny vulnerable people secure right to the land, easy enough to identify those who replicate the role of Babylon in taking land from its inhabitants.

1. We may begin with the colonization of the "New World" by European powers in the fifteenth century. In 1493, a year after Columbus "discovered" America, the pope promulgated "the Doctrine of Discovery," a decree that gave European colonial powers the right to seize the land of the New World, a right that was based on the presumed superiority of white Europeans. The papal decree was subsequently read into U.S. law by the Supreme Court and has since been the ground for the seizure of land from the vulnerable by whites. (See, for example, the Supreme Court ruling in *Johnson v. McIntosh* in 1823.)

2. Black people were disenfranchised and forcibly removed from Forsyth County, Georgia, in the twentieth century.[1] White people simply paid property tax on the vacated land for a period and then became the owners of the land without any purchase of the property. The Black population was simply erased.

3. Federal policy under Franklin Roosevelt supplied tax money to farmers that was locally administered.[2] Predictably, local administrators gave the funds only to white farmers. As Black farmers became increasingly indebted, they lost the land to white farmers, who had money from the federal grants, to secure the land. The outcome was massive land loss for Black farmers.

4. More recently, in an appeal to the right of eminent domain, President Trump urged his staff to "take the land" along the U.S.-Mexican border that was necessary in order to build his promised border wall.[3] The owners of the land likely could not withstand the exercise of the right of eminent domain.

These are all cases of the way in which the powerful violently seize the land of the vulnerable, to which many other examples could be cited. These examples are replays of the world of Jeremiah; all of these agents of seizure play the role of Babylon in land displacement. In every case, the vulnerable who cannot resist such force are left landless. It is easy to see why the great promises of land restoration in chapter 32 would be compelling for those who have lost the land. Biblical faith is the expectation that land will be restored to proper ownership and habitation. Such an expectation, now as then, is surely an "impossibility" to which the displaced may cling in hope-filled desperation. The story of *land loss and displacement* can be reiterated endlessly, not least in the present force of gentrification.

It is not as easy to exposit replications of the *restoration of the land* that is the anticipation of Jeremiah. It is clear that the expectation of land restoration is fueled by the resolve of YHWH. It is clear, moreover, that the Torah of Israel, in its specification of Jubilee, made provision for restoration of lost land. The Torah provision of Jubilee brings to the restoration of lost land not only the resolve of YHWH but the force of law as well:

> If anyone of your kin falls into difficulty and sells a piece of property, then the next of kin shall come and redeem what the relative has sold. . . . But if there is not sufficient means to recover it, what was sold shall remain with the purchaser until the year of jubilee; in the jubilee it shall be released, and the property shall be returned. (Leviticus 25:25, 28)

In our text, Jeremiah plays the role of redeemer of the lost land.

In addition to *the resolve of YHWH* and *the force of the Torah*, we may recognize that land restoration is not an act of magic. It is rather an act of political realism and resolve. In the case of Jeremiah it is the figure of Cyrus the Persian who makes restoration of the land possible. The great decree of Cyrus for restoration to the land is linked to the words of Jeremiah:

> In the first year of King Cyrus of Persia, in fulfillment of the word of the LORD spoken by Jeremiah, the LORD stirred up the spirit of King Cyrus of Persia so that he sent a herald throughout all his kingdom and also declared in a written edict: "Thus says King Cyrus of Persia. . . ." (2 Chronicles 36:22)

We may judge, moreover, that this statement concerning the decree of Cyrus is a reference back to the promise of chapter 32 as well as the promise in 29:10–14.

In the contemporary context of persons facing land seizure (as in the cases cited above) we may ask what sociopolitical resolve is indispensable for the act of land restoration to the vulnerable. In a word, the resolve is provision for *reparations* for those who have been robbed of their land. In the United States, it is *reparations* for slavery that robbed many not only of land but of their bodies and the capacity for a life of dignity and security. Of course, reparations pose all sorts of complex problems. But the practical problems of restoration and reparations are easy enough to solve if there is sufficient political resolve. If the biblical promises are to be taken seriously, then the actual work of restoration is a task that falls to those who care about justice, who read Torah carefully, and who trust the restorative resolve of the faithful God. Restoration from land loss is no pie-in-the-sky fantasy. It is rather an anticipation that God's rule will come on earth as it is in heaven through the serious investment of imaginative political and economic energy. I have cited these contemporary matters in order that we may more fully appreciate what a breathtaking promise the word of Jeremiah was among those who lived with land loss in his ancient world.

Questions for Discussion

1. Do you know of other examples of land seizure?

2. What would land restoration look like now?

3. Is there a contemporary parallel to Jeremiah's purchase of the field?

Chapter 19

A Righteous Branch
(Jeremiah 33:15)

*In those days and at that time I will cause a righteous Branch
to spring up for David; and he shall execute justice and righteousness in the land.*

Scripture Passages for Reference

Jeremiah 21:12, 15–16
Jeremiah 23:5–6
Jeremiah 41:1
Deuteronomy 17:14–20
Isaiah 11:4–5
Psalm 72
Luke 7:22

In the ancient world, the prophetic word inescapably came face-
to-face with royal power. So it is with Jeremiah. At the outset, his
ministry is situated in the royal timeline (1:3). We have seen how
he critiqued King Jehoiakim (22:11–19; see also 36:20–26) and
how he grieved King Jehoiachin (Coniah; 22:28–30), and later on
he will negotiate with King Zedekiah (37:1–10, 17–21; 38:14–28).
While tension was acute between the *inherent interest of the king*
and the *alternative vision of social reality* by the prophet, Jeremiah
never opposed kingship in principle. Rather, he held the monarchy

to the rigorous norms of the Sinai covenant (on which see Deuteronomy 17:14–20).

As the city of Jerusalem was razed by the Babylonians in 587 BCE, a new character, Ishmael, abruptly appears in the book of Jeremiah. In 41:1 Ishmael is said to be "of the royal family." This solitary note might indicate that amid the disaster of 587 BCE there continued to be a lively advocacy for the restoration of the Davidic monarchy that the Babylonians had brutally ended. Ishmael's ignominious mission was to assassinate Gedaliah (of a pro-Babylonian family), who had been made governor of Judah by the Babylonians. His act of assassination was an effort to defeat Babylonian control belatedly and so to make room for the restoration of the monarchy. I cite this assault by Ishmael in order to recognize that there was a continuing pro-David opinion in Jerusalem, even after the termination of the monarchy as a source of governance. While such restoration may have been an illusionary hope, it was strong enough to evoke trouble for the political order of the city.

Given that continuing advocacy and turmoil, we may consider the texts in which Jeremiah addresses the monarchy and summons the royal house to exercise responsible covenantal leadership. While these addresses to monarchy may have been uttered during the time of the monarchy, it is more likely that they look into the future and the possible restoration of monarchy. (In the long run, the church's claim that Jesus is the "anointed" Messiah is a claim that he fulfills the restoration of the royal promise, as he is called "Son of David"; see Mark 10:47–48).

Before taking up our text we may mention three other texts that voice the same hope concerning a restored monarchy. First, in 21:12 the prophetic utterance is addressed generically to the "house of David," making it applicable in every circumstance. The prophetic imperative to the royal house is twofold: "Execute justice . . . and deliver." The proper work of the royal government is to ensure economic justice and viability for those who have been left behind or cheated out of security and dignity by the mechanisms of a predatory economy. That is the proper work of government! As we will see, the prophetic tag word for kingship is "justice," the generation and protection of a viable life of security and dignity for every inhabitant. The "or else" of verse 12 is a recognition that when monarchy fails in this mandate, it is engaged in "evil doings" that will bring violent destruction. In prophetic reasoning, the signal guarantee of social well-being is economic justice, and that is the proper work of the king.

Second, in Jeremiah 22:15–16, we have seen that King Josiah, the father, is celebrated as one who did "justice and righteousness" for the "poor and needy." In addition to "justice," which is the guarantee of economic viability, Jeremiah uses the second term "righteousness," a word that refers to practical actions that restore social health in the neighborhood. In this poem, the son, Jehoiakim, is exactly accused of *in*-justice and *un*-righteousness, actions and policies concerning low wages for workers or wage theft from vulnerable workers (v. 13).

Third, in 23:5–6, there is an anticipation of a new David, a "Branch" from the stump of the royal family. The same imagery is more familiar to us in Isaiah 11:1. In that text as well, it is said of the hoped-for king:

> With righteousness he shall judge the poor,
> and decide with equity for the meek of the earth.
> . . . .
> Righteousness shall be the belt around his waist,
> and faithfulness the belt around his loins.
> Isaiah 11:4–5

In Jeremiah the anticipated king is to execute justice and righteousness—that is, guarantee social viability and commit acts of neighborly restoration. The phrase "deal wisely" (Jeremiah 23:5) might be reminiscent of King Solomon, who is summoned to be wise and who is saluted for his wisdom:

> "Your wisdom and prosperity far surpass the report that I had heard. . . . Because the LORD loved Israel forever, he has made you king to execute justice and righteousness." (1 Kings 10:7, 9)

Of course, Solomon was spectacularly foolish and betrayed his assignment of justice and righteousness. In Jeremiah's words there is hope that the new king will enact the wisdom that Solomon did not do. Such wisdom consists exactly in justice and righteousness, just as royal foolishness consists in injustice and unrighteousness. The new king will act differently, and by such actions Judah will be made safe and Israel will live in safety.

The sum of these three texts makes clear that prophetic imagination contradicts present social reality and hosts the prospect for an alternative governance. The work of governance is justice and righteousness, the protection of the vulnerable from the disastrous avarice of the powerful. That mandate of course is not a prophetic invention. When we consider Psalm 72, no doubt a staple of the royal liturgy, it is exactly affirmed that the primary business of kingship is justice and righteousness:

> Give the king your *justice*, O God,
>   and your *righteousness* to a king's son.
> May he judge your people with *righteousness*,
>   and your poor with *justice*.
> . . . .
> May he defend the cause of the poor of the people,
>   give deliverance to the needy,
>   and crush the oppressor.
> . . . .
> For he delivers the needy when they call,
>   the poor and those who have no helper.
> He has pity on the weak and the needy,
>   and saves the lives of the needy.
>   Psalm 72:1–2, 4, 12–13

That is the proper business of governance! Such policy and practice, moreover, will make the regime safe. And in poetic idiom, that neighborly practice will encourage economic prosperity and cause the earth to function in its proper generativity. To the extent—a very large extent—that climate change is humanly caused, we can see how human injustice and human unrighteousness can disrupt the fruitful ordering of creation. We know this as we witness deforestation, overfishing of our waters, fracking, and excessive reliance on fossil fuels, all of which help to make the earth an unlivable habitat. The biblical witness of course is prescientific, but it witnesses to the truth about the linkage of *human justice* and *fruitful creation*.

When we finally come to Jeremiah 33:14, the phrasing is by now familiar to us and expected. The book of Jeremiah, for all of its articulation of divine judgment against Jerusalem, is elementally a book of hope that anticipates YHWH's generous planting and building—not just the trek into exile but also the long, hard return back from that abyss. The opening phrase of this verse, "The days are coming," is a characteristic prophetic trope indicating that God's sure future will be quite unlike the present. That future will not be extrapolated from the present but will appear by a fresh initiative from the creator God. For the prophet that coming future is certain, but without a timetable of prediction. In that coming sure future, there will be a new Davidic king. That king, moreover, will be unlike those kings known in the present, though perhaps King Josiah is a foretaste of the quality of the coming king. The world will be under new management; that new management, however, will not be by some spectacular supernaturalism. It will be, rather, an actual institutional governance not defined by wealth, power, and wisdom, but by justice, mercy, and righteousness (Jeremiah 9:23–24).

Jews and Christians together share hope for such a Coming One. Judaism trusts that "Messiah will come." Christians confess that in Jesus of Nazareth we have already seen the exhibit of God's intended governance, for Jesus did indeed go about doing justice, righteousness, and mercy: "'The blind receive their sight, the lame walk, the lepers are cleansed, the deaf hear, the dead are raised, the poor have good news brought to them'" (Luke 7:22). It is certain, moreover, that Jesus' evident commitment to justice, righteousness, and mercy put him on a collision course with the rulers of the day, so that Jesus had to be executed as an enemy of the status quo (see Matthew 23:23–24).

For all of that, however, Christians still wait (alongside Jews) for the full coming of the rule of God that Jesus has exhibited and enacted. Thus finally the New Testament concludes with expectation that contradicts the status quo but at the same time readily acknowledges that we do not now have such governance in God's earth: "Amen. Come, Lord Jesus!" (Revelation 22:20). Given that prayer concerning God's future, Jews and Christians hope together for the coming governance. This means that Jews and Christians refuse to accept "standard operating procedures" of money and power as normative, and refuse to believe that things will always be the way they are. This coming governance will be, we confess, radically different. It is no wonder that this promised future is so welcomed by those presently left behind. Nor is it a wonder that those who benefit most from the present unjust, unrighteous status quo will go to great lengths to resist the newness.

Seen in this way, this promissory oracle of Jeremiah is a call to decide: either for the continuing status quo of injustice and unrighteousness, or for the coming alternative of justice and righteousness. Such prophetic hope is not only an assurance. It is a summons. The book of Jeremiah intends that its readers should bet on the future and be engaged for it. Shorn of its historical connections, we may take the familiar hymn as a summons for the faithful to walk boldly into that coming, God-given future:

> Mine eyes have seen the glory of the coming of the Lord;
> he is trampling out the vintage where the grapes of wrath are
>   stored;
> he has loosed the fateful lightning of his terrible swift sword.
> God's truth is marching on.[1]

Jeremiah is preoccupied with this march of God's truth; after tearing down and plucking up, YHWH is about the real-world work of planting and building.

Questions for Discussion

1. Where do you see a connection between human justice and fruitful creation?

2. What is the proper work of government in your opinion? In Jeremiah's?

3. How might we refuse the standard operating procedures of money and power?

4. Where do you see planting and building taking place? Or, if you see no traces of that, where might it be possible and imaginable?

Chapter 20

Many Similar Words
(Jeremiah 36:32)

Then Jeremiah took another scroll and gave it to the secre-
tary Baruch son of Neriah, who wrote on it at Jeremiah's
dictation all the words of the scroll that King Jehoiakim of
Judah had burned in the fire; and many similar words were
added to them.

Scripture Passages for Reference

Jeremiah 7:5–7
Jeremiah 26:2–6
Jeremiah 36
2 Kings 22:8

It is evident that Jeremiah's "original" word to the power elite of
Jerusalem was an echo of the transactional theology of the book of
Deuteronomy (see 30:15–20):

Keep Torah—live and prosper.
Disobey Torah—suffer adversity and die.

In Jeremiah that quid pro quo reasoning results in a series of prophetic speeches of judgment constituted by *indictments* for Torah
failures and *sentences* that implement covenant curses. Jeremiah's

early *poetic utterances* are very much to this point. That same reasoning, moreover, is evident in the *narrative reports* of public confrontations undertaken by the prophet. In Jeremiah's "temple sermon," the prophet states the conditionality of the covenant in a series of if-then statements that depend on covenantal obedience (Jeremiah 7:5–7). This conditionality then segues in the chapter to a harsh indictment for a failed political economy. The same themes are sounded in the narrative introduction to Jeremiah's "trial" in 26:2–6 with the same if-then conditionality of covenantal assumptions. As in the temple sermon, the hope of the prophet is that his listeners will turn from their evil ways in order to avoid the historical disaster that disobedience will surely evoke. The inescapable conclusion of this line of reasoning with the hope of a "turn" (conversion) is that Jerusalem is on a course to disaster because its policies and its practices contradict the intent of YHWH. In prophetic horizon it is clear that the power elite in Jerusalem had disregarded Torah, likely in the conviction that YHWH had made an unconditional commitment to king, temple, and city, so that disaster and deportation were not possible for Jerusalem's assured future. The point of Jeremiah's utterance was to warn the city and to expose the toxic policies to which the Jerusalem elite were firmly committed.

Now in chapter 36, the Jeremiah tradition makes an enormous move from *oral utterance* to *written testimony*. This transition that was defining for early Judaism was at the behest of YHWH, who authorized scroll-making, whereby the tradition of Israel morphed into the reality of written Torah (36:2). We know very little about how any book of the Old Testament came to be. But chapter 36 provides for us a clue about the origin of the book of Jeremiah. We have seen in 1:1 that the book of Jeremiah is constituted by "the words of Jeremiah." Here, by contrast, it is said that Jeremiah dictated the words spoken by YHWH and received by Jeremiah. If we consider the tension between the claim of 1:1 and that of 36:2–5, we can see the endless trickiness in adjudicating exactly the relationship between "the word of the LORD" and the scroll, and therefore the trickiness of claims about "biblical authority."

That, however, is not the issue that preoccupies Jeremiah or his secretary, Baruch. They are quite willing to leave such a question open and unresolved. What concerns them, rather, is the purpose of the scroll now being dictated. The purpose of their work is to evoke repentance in Jerusalem in order to avert the coming disaster:

> . . . all of them may *turn* from their evil ways, so that I may forgive their iniquity and their sin. . . . "It may be that their plea will come before the LORD, and that all of them will *turn* from their evil ways, for great is the anger and wrath that the LORD has pronounced against this people." (vv. 3, 7)

There is immense urgency to this appeal, but there is also an unmistakable judgment that the present governance in Jerusalem is wrongheaded and can only bring trouble. While the rhetoric of the prophetic utterance depends upon the agency of YHWH as judge who will intrude into public affairs, little imagination is required to see that the mistaken policies themselves contain within them the seeds of disaster. Thus the work of Jeremiah, by *utterance* and by *scroll*, is to place before the elite of the city the most elemental either-or of life or death that no amount of denial or illusion can nullify.

We may trace the dramatic account of this narrative chapter in four steps. First, there is the process whereby the scroll that Baruch wrote worked its way into the attention of the king. That process entailed (a) a public reading of the scroll in the temple (v. 10), (b) the detaining and quizzing of Baruch by officials of the royal government (v. 17), and (c) another reading in the presence of the king's cabinet (v. 21). After some interrogation, the officials recognized that the scroll that Baruch had written—that declared Jerusalem to be in imminent danger—was in fact itself a high-risk offer. They knew that the scroll would evoke the aggressive hostility of the king. Their counsel to Baruch suggests that the officials had both great resonance with the scroll and great concern for the well-being of its authors. Imagine, if you can, being an advisor to a political leader while you are convinced of the foolishness of his policies! These royal advisors wanted the scroll to be presented to the king, but without excessive exposure for its progenitors. As a result, their counsel to Baruch and Jeremiah is "Go and hide," for the pair will be seen by the king to be enemies of the state (v. 19).

Second, the scroll finally arrives at the royal suite. The narrative is at pains to make the moment of *scroll versus king* as specific and as dramatic as possible. Jehudi clearly is the king's closest and most trusted advisor; now he must read the dangerous scroll to the king (v. 21).

This is the moment of confrontation. The prophetic scroll receives a hearing by the king! This dramatic moment is (intentionally?) a parallel to the moment when his father, King Josiah, had heard the scroll (2 Kings 22:8). While Josiah took the scroll (of Deuteronomy) with great seriousness, Jehoiakim (see Jeremiah 22:13–19) mocks the scroll and dismisses it with contempt (Jeremiah 36:23–25). The king shreds the document; he imagines that by disposing of the scroll he will dispose of the alleged threat voiced by the prophet. Whereas Josiah "tore his clothes" in repentance (2 Kings 22:11), Jehoiakim "tears" (the same word) the scroll to bits in his contempt (Jeremiah 36:23). His disdain for the scroll arises from his disdain for the Torah tradition, for the claims of covenant and for the God of covenant. It is clear that the contempt of the king is grounded in his dismay that Jeremiah could anticipate that the king of Babylon would come as a threat against Jerusalem (v. 30). This episode of contempt ends with the terse note concerning Jeremiah and Baruch, now sought by a royal posse: "The LORD hid them" (v. 26). We may imagine that while it is YHWH who hid them, YHWH was helped by human agents who supported the prophet's view of social and historical reality; they knew that the king was on a path of self-destruction, even while they remained in his service. Specifically we may judge that it was the family of Shaphan that provided protection for the prophet and Baruch (see 26:24).

Our interest, however, is in the fourth moment in the drama, which takes place after the royal shredding of the document (vv. 27–32). In verse 28 Jeremiah is commanded by YHWH to "take another scroll," a command he obeys in verse 32. He again dictates his words to Baruch. The God who authorized the new scroll is undeterred by royal resistance. It is, so says the text, YHWH's own word that persists against Jehoiakim (see 22:18–19) and that reiterates the coming disaster against Jerusalem, because "they would not listen" (v. 31). Remarkably, an additional note is included: "And many similar words were added" to this new and improved (extended, expanded, edited) scroll.

This dramatic confrontation between *scroll* and *king* might have ended in royal triumph with the king shredding the prophetic document. Perhaps Jehoiakim thought he had prevailed and had defeated the scroll and its authors. If so, however, the king greatly underestimated the resolve of Baruch who wrote the scroll, the resolve of Jeremiah who dictated the scroll, and the resolve of YHWH who authorized the scroll. What a triad of scroll-makers these three are! Together they constitute a force of truth-telling resolve before which the king, in his foolish illusion, is helpless.

Taken historically, the production of "another scroll" likely bears witness to the dynamic processes whereby the book of Jeremiah came into existence. We may judge that there was a series of such productions, editions, or redactions. Certainly current scholarship judges that there are a variety of voices and advocacies in the text. Indeed, the book of Jeremiah in its complexity becomes an arena for the vigorous contestation that beset the troubled city and the vexed tradition-making of Jeremiah's circle. Thus the book of Jeremiah came into being by an ordering of sequenced editions that are beyond our knowledge. We may be glad that "more words were added," because surely added among them were the words of great hope for restored Jerusalem and the return of the deportees that served the future of Judaism.

Taken theologically, we can see that the Israelite-Jewish tradition is text-formed and text-based in a relentless and resilient process of text-making, text-transmitting, and text-interpreting, a process that kings cannot stop or resist. It is a process that refuses the closure of any final reading, because final readings inevitably lead to final solutions. For good reason Robert Alter has declared that Judaism is a "culture of interpretation." And for equally good reason George Steiner has seen that "the text" was "the instrument of exilic survival" that offered "an unhoused at-homeness." When Israel was deported from its land it could carry with it the text, and for that reason it could celebrate and rely on a belonging that the king—king of Judah or king of Babylon—could not nullify. The elusive availability of the text will endlessly reassert historical possibility intended by the author of the text and so defeat the history-ending absolutism of royal or imperial anxiety. Thus George Steiner, in his eloquence, can declare:

> The truth will out. Somewhere there is a pencil-stub, a mimeograph machine, a hand-press which the king's men have overlooked. . . .

The Temple may be destroyed; the texts which it housed sing in the winds that scatter them.[1]

We may read chapter 36 with a double vision. On the one hand, we may linger over the scroll-king confrontation in which the king cannot win, not even with his ready violence. On the other hand, we may take a larger view about the vitality of the text, the endlessly enigmatic "authority of Scripture" and what it means to have this lively text entrusted to us. The text summons us to be its responsible adherents and attentive custodians. The biblical text, of which Jeremiah 36 is a harbinger, has endless vitality; both the synagogue and the church return to it endlessly and find fresh dimension through interpretation. When the ancient canonizing process seemed finished, the adding of "many similar words" (see verse 32) has continued through the never-ending work of interpretation. We are always learning again what Jeremiah, Baruch, and Jehoiakim had to learn—that "God is still speaking." We, like the king, refuse to listen at our great peril. As the apostle has written of Jesus' actions, "If every one of them were written down, I suppose that the world itself could not contain the books that would be written" (John 21:25).

Jeremiah is an urgent witness to the claim that there are "many similar words" yet to be received by the faithful.

Questions for Discussion

1. Where do you see other examples of text-making, text-transmitting, and text-interpreting? How is the community of faith still involved in those processes?

2. Do you agree that "truth will out"? Why or why not?

3. How does God still speak, and how is that related to "the scroll" that is Scripture?

Chapter 21

There Is a Word from the Lord, Unfortunately (Jeremiah 37:17)

The King Zedekiah sent for him, and received him. The king questioned him secretly in his house, and said, "Is there any word from the LORD?" Jeremiah said, "There is!" Then he said, "You shall be handed over to the king of Babylon."

Scripture Passages for Reference
Jeremiah 38:14–28
2 Samuel 7:15–16
Psalm 89:35–37

Jeremiah 37–39 provides a narrative account of the last days of the Davidic monarchy in Jerusalem. It traverses the final decade of the Davidic dynasty occupied by the last king, Zedekiah (see 1:3). That decade began in 598 BCE when Nebuchadnezzar deported the boy king Jehoiachin (see 2 Kings 24:8–12) and lasted until the final deportation of Zedekiah in chains in 587 (Jeremiah 39:7). This is, however, no ordinary historical account of monarchy, because the narrative pivots around the prophetic word of Jeremiah. Indeed, his prophetic utterance is regarded in the narrative as crucially constitutive for the history of Jerusalem.

The immediate threat of Babylon looms over the entire narrative. Jerusalem had already experienced the first onslaught of Babylon in

598, but that initial invasion had not abated the continuing threat of the empire. Zedekiah, already at the beginning of this narrative, is panic-stricken. He is beyond any possible initiative on his own part. As a move of last resort he petitions Jeremiah to pray for the city (37:3). He does so "secretly" (v. 17). After all, a great king must not be seen consulting with an uncredentialed street poet. But that only indicates how desperate the king is. The secret move by the king is not unlike that of Nicodemus, "a leader of the Jews," who came to see Jesus "by night" (John 3:1). After all, a great interpreter of the Torah has no business seeking out a Galilean street bard. In both cases officialdom is propelled beyond "official wisdom" when official wisdom has been shown to be phony and ineffective. The drama is staged in the narrative to exhibit the claim that the monarchy is penultimate and must finally acknowledge that "the word of the LORD" is effectively operative even in and beyond the royal domain. The king seeks the petition of the prophet to YHWH. He has in mind more than something like, "Our thoughts and prayers are with you." He hopes that the prayers of the prophet might be efficacious in mobilizing YHWH to deliver him and his regime from the Babylonian threat. Zedekiah was apparently unaware that YHWH had prohibited Jeremiah from praying for this people (7:16; 11:24; 14:11). Jeremiah does not respond to the royal request for prayer but reiterates his programmatic concern about the ominous return of Babylon against the city (37:8–10).

When his request for a prayer of deliverance is disregarded, Zedekiah, beset by immense anxiety, asks the prophet if he has a word from YHWH. He asks in hope, assuming that a word from YHWH (any word!) will be reassuring because YHWH has long been the patron and guarantor of the city and the dynasty. The king hopes and assumes that the word will echo the ancient promise to David (2 Samuel 7:15–16) that was liturgically reiterated in hymnic form:

"Once and for all I have sworn by my holiness;
    I will not lie to David.
His line shall continue forever,
    and his throne endure before me like the sun.
It shall be established forever like the moon,
    an enduring witness in the skies."
Psalm 89:35–37

Jeremiah's answer to Zedekiah is terse, but the king takes it as reassuring: "There is!" Yes, the prophet has a word for the king. We may imagine that there was a long pause before the next prophetic statement. In that pause the king must have been greatly expectant. Likely Jeremiah paused because he did not relish the next words he had to speak to the king; what he had to say dashed the hope of the king and contradicted the long-term claim of the dynasty on the unconditional faithfulness of YHWH. Finally, Jeremiah continues. His next words voice the sum of his theme, which is a combination of *theological conviction* and *geopolitical realism*: "You shall be handed over to the king of Babylon." That word from Jeremiah gave notice to the king and the nation that YHWH's resolve had moved on from unconditional promise to David to sovereign impatience toward YHWH's own chosen people, king, and city. They had now become objects of sovereign judgment. His unexpected word to the king caused Jeremiah to be promptly labeled as a traitor who was undermining the war effort (38:4). That encounter between king and prophet ends with Zedekiah's attentive gesture concerning the personal well-being of Jeremiah (37:20–21). It is evident that king and prophet are not simply adversaries; their relationship is more complex than that, as together they face the bewilderment of an ominous future for their city.

The terse "There is!" of Jeremiah in 37:17 leads to a continuing interaction between king and prophet. In their second exchange, their conversation advances (38:14–28). The coming of Babylon against Jerusalem is no longer contested. Now the question is how to respond to the Babylonian threat. There are only two options: *resist* or *submit*. Jeremiah is unambiguous. In his double if-then statement in verses 17–18, he urges the king to surrender and face up to geopolitical reality that he sees as the will of YHWH as well.

If you surrender,

Then your life will be spared.

If you do not surrender,

Then this city will be handed over to the Chaldeans.

His statement receives no response from the king. The encounter ends with the king and prophet together preparing a "press release" that in fact covers over the harsh truth that Jeremiah has spoken. We can see here, as in 37:20–22, that beyond their formal opposition, king and prophet have a continuing capacity for human interaction. We can see, moreover, that for all of his boldness, Jeremiah has concern for his personal safety. The king as well is able to address personal issues in the midst of dreadful public reality.

In the end the king does not heed the word of the prophet. He imagines that his own policy of resistance, without reference to the will of YHWH or the wisdom of the prophet, can succeed. It is evident that the royal government resisted Babylon or there would not have been the fierce seizure of the city by the Babylonians (38:1–3), nor would the king have fled in fear (38:4–5). Zedekiah refused to submit; he opted for the second if-then of verse 18:

> "*If* you do not surrender to the officials of the king of Babylon, *then* this city shall be handed over to the Chaldeans, and they shall burn it with fire, and you yourself shall not escape from their hand."

In his warning to the king, Jeremiah doubles down on the hard ending of the "then" for Zedekiah's regime:

> "All your wives and your children shall be led out to the Chaldeans, and you yourself shall not escape from their hand, but shall be seized by the king of Babylon; and this city shall be burned with fire." (v. 23)

The ending for the king was as brutal as can be imagined. Zedekiah had to witness the execution of his sons, who were the heirs to the throne (39:6). It was as though Nebuchadnezzar wanted to make the brutality against the city as final as he possibly could. Zedekiah ends up in chains with the deportation of the entire royal entourage. The scene is one of violent humiliation before which the ancient dynasty of David, with its ancient promises from YHWH, counted for nil— for nothing with Babylonian power, and for nothing with YHWH's covenantal-transactional reasoning.

The sum of 37:1–39:10 amounts to a vindication of the word of Jeremiah. He had from the outset seen that YHWH's historical purpose was being embodied and worked out through Babylon; see already an anticipatory allusion to Babylon (1:13; 5:15–17; 6:22–23). Jeremiah had further judged that the future of Israel would be carried by those who had heeded his word and submitted to deportation and exile (24:1–10). He had seen that resistance to Babylon ran counter to the grain of history and so counter to the will of the Lord of history.

Two themes invite reflection in these chapters. First, we may consider the matter of Jeremiah's personal life and well-being. We do not often reflect on what the personal life of a bold public advocate must be like. We do not consider very much what it was like for Bonhoeffer to linger in a Nazi prison or what it was like for Oscar Romero to look up at the altar and see his killer right in front of him. Self-regard does not disappear with an acute sense of vocation. And so Jeremiah pleads with the king not to send him to prison (37:20), fears he will be put to death by the king (38:15), colludes with the king in a misleading press release (38:24–28), and finally receives a "safe conduct" from the victorious Nebuchadnezzar (39:11–18).

But the countertheme that crosses paths with personal self-concern is the relentless sovereign truth of YHWH's rule over the nations. The stark "There is!" to the king is an affirmation that the word of YHWH cannot be trimmed or tailored to suit the power elite. There is a way in history, attests the prophet, that does not conform to our best hopes or our vested interests. The prophetic task embraced by Jeremiah is to bear witness to that overriding purpose that is implemented in ways that mock our best reason and our best hope.

Questions for Discussion

1. What do you make of the if-then dynamic in this passage of Jeremiah?

2. Have you thought much of the word of the Lord as a negative phenomenon?

3. What cost accompanies a Christian calling?

4. Is it hard for you to believe in "the relentless sovereign truth of YHWH's rule over the nations"?

Chapter 22

Mercy Shown (or Not)
(Jeremiah 42:11–12)

*Do not be afraid of the king of Babylon, as you have been;
do not be afraid of him, says the LORD, for I am with you, to
save you and to rescue you from his hand. I will grant you
mercy, and he will have mercy on you and restore you to
your native soil.*

Scripture Passages for Reference

Jeremiah 6:22–23
Jeremiah 21:7
Jeremiah 26:24
Jeremiah 42:1
Jeremiah 43:1–7
2 Kings 25:26

The extended narrative of Jeremiah 37–45 divides into two fairly
symmetrical parts. As we have seen, chapters 37–39 detail the final
decade of the monarchy and the ignoble, brutal ending of King
Zedekiah. The other half of the narrative, chapters 40–44, concerns
the social dismay and confusion after the collapse of the monarchy.
(Chapter 45 is a reprise of the whole.) In the second half of this narrative, it should not surprise us that there is severe disputation, as

different parties of advocacy compete to take control of sociopolitical reality and social vision.

We can identify three powerful opinions that are operative in the narrative. First, there is the *pro-Babylonian party* for which Jeremiah is a spokesperson. This party believed that the wise course was to submit to the overwhelming power of Babylon. In Jeremiah's reading, moreover, practical judgment was articulated as the will for YHWH for the safety of Judah and Jerusalem, as they could not withstand the Babylonian Empire. That party came to provisional power as Gedaliah, the heir of the important family of Shaphan, was appointed by Babylon as governor of what was now a Babylonian province (see 26:24). (Seen from a different perspective, Gedaliah could be viewed as a quisling, a traitor who colluded with foreign interests.)

Second, there was a party that wanted to get as far away from Babylon as possible and so fled to Egypt at the other end of the international map of the time. We are told very little of this movement; we know that it was led by Johanan son of Kereah and Azariah son of Hoshaiah (42:1). What we know of this group is from the critical perspective of the book of Jeremiah that reads the *Egyptian option* as an act of unforgivable disobedience to the will of YHWH. Thus its leaders are termed "insolent" (43:2). Of course, if one begins with the Babylonian option, then any flight to Egypt is out of the question. In an act most repellent to him, Jeremiah, against his will, is forced to go to Egypt (43:1–7; see 2 Kings 25:26). Jeremiah's verdict against this coerced deportation, voiced in 43:1–7, is that no one can finally escape the reach of Nebuchadnezzar, whose power will devastate Egypt:

> He shall kindle a fire in the temples of the gods of Egypt; and he shall burn them and carry them away captive; and he shall pick clean the land of Egypt, as a shepherd picks his cloak clean of vermin; and he shall depart from there safely. (43:12)

The prophetic word against Jews in Egypt is savage and final:

> I will take the remnant of Judah who are determined to come to the land of Egypt to settle, and they shall perish, everyone; in the land of Egypt they shall fall; by the sword and by famine they shall perish; from the least to the greatest, they shall die by the sword

and by famine, and they shall become an object of execration and horror, of cursing and ridicule. . . . "I am going to watch over them for harm and not for good; all the people of Judah who are in the land of Egypt shall perish by the sword and by famine, until not one is left." (44:12, 27)

We know from archaeological sources that a significant Jewish community did survive and prosper in Egypt. Indeed, it was this community that eventually produced the Septuagint, the translation of the Hebrew Bible into Greek. From the perspective of Babylonian Jews, however, this Egyptian community was religiously heterodox and unacceptable, straying from the norms of Torah obedience.

The Egyptian community of Jews, in the purview of Jeremiah, was summarily dismissed. We know, moreover, that only a small number of Jews were carried away to Babylon. That select community, however, came to exercise a strong influence on emergent Judaism. Given these two communities in Egypt and Babylon, we can recognize that the great majority of the population of Judah, constituting a third opinion, *remained in the land*. It is evident in 41:1 that within that remaining population there was an active opinion, led by Ishmael, son of Nethaniah, that hoped and continued to contend for the restoration of the Davidic monarchy. That remaining community, moreover, is thought to be represented by the book of Lamentations, a community left in grief by loss and devastation.

Our first task is to see that the future of Judaism and the destiny of Israel were highly contested among these three groups. But what interests us is that Jeremiah vigorously weighs in on this much-contested issue of the future of the Jewish population. In the midst of this confusion, leaders Johanan and Azariah ask Jeremiah to pray for "this remnant" of remaining Jews. They not only ask for prayer (in the same way that King Zedekiah had earlier asked of Jeremiah; 42:2) but also promise to accept Jeremiah's guidance:

> "Whether it is good or bad, we will obey the voice of the LORD our God to whom we are sending you, in order that it may go well with us when we obey the voice of the LORD our God." (42:6)

In his response to their request, Jeremiah delivers another *if-then* declaration that is an echo of the if-then he had earlier stated to King

Zedekiah. The rhetorical form is closely parallel to 38:17–18. But the substance has changed with the changed circumstance:

> "*If* you will only remain in this land, *then* I will build you up and not pull you down; I will plant you, and not pluck you up." (42:10)

In this remarkable utterance, the prophet utilizes the four verbs of his initial call from YHWH. Now the two positive verbs of restoration (plant, build) override the two negative verbs of displacement (pluck up, tear down). The news is good, but it is conditioned by remaining in the land—that is, refusing to flee to Egypt. Thus Jeremiah clings to the Babylonian option; only now the way to submit to Babylon is to remain quietly in the land without resistance. This simple *if-then* construct is followed by an assurance that YHWH will grant mercy to those who comply; the mercy of YHWH, moreover, will be matched by the mercy of Babylon (vv. 11–12)! This remarkable statement anticipates that the mighty brutal superpower of Babylon will be a practitioner of God's mercy.

We should note that in a subsequent text, that same Babylon is chastened by Isaiah because YHWH had given Babylon carte blanche against Israel; the empire had acted brutally and showed "no mercy":

> I was angry with my people.
> . . . .
> I gave them into your hand,
>   you showed them *no mercy*;
> on the aged you made your yoke
>   exceedingly heavy.
> Isaiah 47:6

The remarkable assurance of 42:12 is even more astonishing because elsewhere Jeremiah has said otherwise. Thus in 6:22–23, in an allusion to Babylon, Jeremiah anticipated:

> See, a people is coming from the land of the north,
> . . . .
> They grasp the bow and the javelin,
>   they are cruel and have *no mercy*.

And in 21:7, Jeremiah anticipates Babylonian brutality:

He [Nebuchadnezzar] shall not pity them, or spare them, or have compassion [mercy].

Thus the assurance of 42:11–12 does not evoke much confidence; Jeremiah's word was, moreover, rejected by those who had made inquiry of him:

> "You are telling a lie. The LORD our God did not send you to say, 'Do not go to Egypt to settle there.'" . . . So Johanan son of Kareah and all the commanders of the forces and all the people did not obey the voice of the LORD, to stay in the land of Judah. (43:2–4)

Jeremiah, however, is adamant. In 42:13–17, he issues a negative *if-then* declaration that matches the positive statement of 42:10. It is noteworthy that this negative if-then formulation does not include the two verbs of displacement: *pluck up* and *tear down*. It does, however, conclude with a stylized articulation of classic curses, the likely residue of violent confrontation: *sword, famine, pestilence* (v. 17).

This narrative comes to a sorry end even as the life of Jeremiah comes to a sorry end. The narrative, as well as Jeremiah, ends in Egypt. Jeremiah is completely at odds with his coerced life in Egypt as he rails against Egypt and against the Jews who required him to be there. It is likely the case, as he pondered his life in Egypt, that the graciousness of Babylon looked all the better to him as the only political alternative to Egypt.

For the most part the rhetoric of these chapters is a torrent of judgment, wrath, and reprimand. For that reason it is all the more astonishing to notice the promise in 42:11–12 that grows out of the if-then of verse 10. In the midst of deportation, conflict, confusion, and turmoil, the prophet manages to utter this word of mercy. He appeals to the mercy of YHWH that he anticipates can well up in the midst of vexed human history. That same positive anticipation also sounds in the Book of Comfort, where the passion of YHWH is declared to the deportees. In 31:20 it is declared that YHWH "will surely have mercy" because YHWH has discovered, in the midst of rage against Israel, that Israel is "my dear son." This anticipation of mercy is voiced in a device of Hebrew grammar that adds intensity, infinitive absolute, making the divine promise even more emphatic. And in 33:26 Jeremiah declares mercy for "the offspring of Abraham, Isaac, and Jacob" that will "restore their fortunes." While we expect the declarations of YHWH's mercy in the Book of Comfort, we surely do not expect them in the later material concerning Egypt and the forced displacement of Jeremiah. But there the reference is! This statement of mercy, human and divine, indicates that even in profound extremity the prophet could not fully get outside the reach of YHWH's mercy that has been affirmed since the initial crisis of the golden calf in the exodus story:

> "The LORD, the LORD,
> a God *merciful* and gracious,
> slow to anger,
> and abounding in steadfast love and faithfulness."
>
> Exodus 34:6

Such an affirmation as offered in our text presents a great wonderment: Can mercy operate in a world of savage power politics? Under the tutelage of Reinhold Niebuhr we are urged to think that in the public sphere we can only hope for justice, while mercy belongs only to interpersonal relationships. But still, the God of mercy is the Lord of history! It is not easy to think of instances of public mercy. We might, however, think of Abraham Lincoln:

> We are not enemies, but friends. We must not be enemies. Though passion may have strained, it must not break our bonds of affection. The mystic chords of memory, stretching from every battlefield, and patriot grave, to every living heart and hearthstone, all over this broad land, will yet swell the chorus of the Union, when again touched, as surely they will be, by the better angels of our nature. (First Inaugural Address)

> With malice toward none; with charity for all; with firmness in the right, as God gives us to see the right, let us strive on to finish the work we are in; to bind up the nation's wounds; to care for him who shall have borne the battle, and for his widow, and his orphan—to do all which may achieve and cherish a just, and lasting peace, among ourselves and with all nations. (Second Inaugural Address)

In our own greatly conflicted political economy, we might wonder how largeness of spirit and generosity might be transformative. Of course, such public acts of mercy are never fully disinterested. They are, however, possible. Even in the throes of danger and defeat, Jeremiah has imagined mercy from a superpower toward a vulnerable people. What a wondrous act of imagination rooted in the God whom he imagined as the God of mercy!

Questions for Discussion

1. Where is mercy shown now?

2. Is it imaginable that mercy might be shown in the public square? In the Christian communion?

3. How and where does God, "who is rich in mercy" (Ephesians 2:4), manifest that mercy? Or not?

Chapter 23

The End(s) of Baruch (Jeremiah 45:5)

"But I will give you your life as a prize of war in every place to which you may go."

Scripture Passages for Reference

Jeremiah 25:30–31
Jeremiah 32:12–16
Jeremiah 36
Jeremiah 43:3–6
Jeremiah 45

The narrative of chapters 37–44 features a double rejection of "the word of the LORD" and a double rebuff to Jeremiah. On the one hand, King Zedekiah refuses the prophetic mandate to submit to Babylon, and he is summarily and brutally deported (39:6–7). On the other hand, some leaders in Judah refuse the prophetic mandate to remain in the land. They flee to Egypt and become the object of an extreme prophetic reprimand (44:1–14). The double rebuff of Jeremiah leaves him without the protection of Babylon that had been on offer and ends with him (and Baruch) in Egypt—the very last place he wanted to be, a place most remote from Babylonian protection. It is no wonder that this long narrative account of failure and demise ends, in chapter 45, with a searing judgment on "the whole land," the land that has resisted the mandate of "the word of the LORD." That harsh judgment on "the whole land" in chapter 45 is intertwined with the personal destiny of Baruch, whom we may take as a representative figure for those who trusted Jeremiah's prophetic word. At the same time, this brief chapter deals with both a verdict on "the whole land" and a different verdict for the faithful few.

This prophetic oracle of chapter 45 is dated to 605 BCE, the fifth year of King Jehoiakim and the first year of Nebuchadnezzar of Babylon. It is as though in that fateful year the future of Judah was decisively fixed with the failure of Jehoiakim and the rise of Nebuchadnezzar. Jeremiah's verdict on public matters is confined to verse 4, with an additional comment in verse 5. It is likely that the scope of this negative judgment is the land of Judah. In that case the divine verdict means that no part of "the land of promise" will escape judgment.

There is, however, an alternative translation of the prophetic phrase concerning the scope of judgment. It is entirely possible that "the whole land" (that is, the land of Judah) can be translated as "the whole earth," referring to the entire international horizon of the day. Such a translation would connect the prophetic word to the more nearly "apocalyptic" vision of 25:30–31:

> The LORD will roar from on high,
>   and from his holy habitation utter his voice
> . . . .
>   against *all the inhabitants of the earth.*
> The clamor will resound to the ends of the earth,
>   for the LORD has an indictment against the nations;
> he is entering into judgment with *all flesh,*
>   and the guilty he will put to the sword,
>   says the LORD.

In these lines, YHWH, a roaring lion, will devastate all nations. The scope of devastation for "all nations" echoes the "over nations" of Jeremiah's call (1:10). The prophet is acutely focused on Jerusalem, but at the same time keeps in purview the international landscape over which, he asserts, YHWH presides. YHWH's rule (and therefore YHWH's judgment) pertains to all nations, including the superpower, Babylon. If we take that translation, then the familiar verbs of 45:4 concern all creation. YHWH had built and planted all the nations. And now, all the nations will be torn down and plucked up. Either translation anticipates a coming devastation, *for Judah* and/or *for the nations*. There is no exception; there is no reservation; there is no escape. A nation (or a world) that lives in contradiction to and defiance of the will of the sovereign God finally will reap the whirlwind of alienation. If we take the more inclusive sense of the phrase "the whole earth," the words provide a fitting segue to chapters 46–51 that concern YHWH's judgment on the nations. That linkage, moreover, is exactly what is given in the Greek translation of the book of Jeremiah, in which chapters 46–51 are placed just after 25:13a. This would place an accent on "all flesh" in 45:5.

Either translation, "land" or "earth," bespeaks an irreversible dev-astation for those who oppose YHWH. Chapter 45, however, is not primarily about this wholesale judgment, as massive as it will be. This oracle, rather, is addressed to Baruch (45:2). Baruch has made three previous appearances in the book of Jeremiah. Most promi-nently, as we have seen, Baruch wrote down the scroll dictated by Jeremiah (chapter 36). He consequently had to go into hiding with Jeremiah (36:26). Before this, in 32:12–16 Baruch is responsible for keeping the deed of title to the land Jeremiah has purchased. And finally, as we have seen, in 43:3–6 Baruch suffers the same fate as Jeremiah and is forced to go to Egypt. In all of these citations Baruch is Jeremiah's loyal adherent and faithful companion. We may, moreover, take Baruch as a representative figure of the small subcommunity in Judah that had trusted Jeremiah and accepted his reading of historical reality. Thus we may understand the prophetic oracle in chapter 45 to be concerned with the destiny of that loyal subcommunity.

The oracle of Jeremiah is a response to the lament of Baruch in verse 3. Baruch is filled with sorrow and pain; he is exhausted and engages in some self-pity. It is surely well-earned self-pity. He has risked everything to follow Jeremiah, and look what it has gotten him! He is disconsolate. Jeremiah's sweeping judgment in verses 4–5 against "all flesh" is perhaps an assurance to Baruch. The viola-tors of YHWH will not get by with their hubris. In the end they will suffer greatly. I suppose this is an invitation to *Schadenfreude* for

Baruch, a chance to "enjoy" the suffering of those at whose hand he has suffered greatly.

But then, in verse 5, YHWH through Jeremiah reprimands Baruch. It is as though Baruch had hope for triumph and an outcome of public well-being for his faithfulness. Perhaps he hoped that with the defeat of old powers he and his ilk would dominate. Maybe that is among the "great things" he had anticipated for himself. YHWH through Jeremiah rebukes Baruch for any such notion, as though to say, "Did you think we would win? Did you imagine our domination in any new era?" Not the case!

After this reprimand, however, the final word to Baruch is one of assurance and affirmation. In the violence that is sure to come, there will be massive dislocation, loss, and suffering. Anything and everyone will be destroyed—all flesh! But then, halfway through verse 5 there is an adversative conjunction, "but." The cosmic sweep of condemnation is interrupted and qualified. There is the prospect of an alternative destiny just for "you," Baruch, you who have been steadfast and reliable! The oracle imagines YHWH walking through the war damage, sorting things out. Everything is ruined. Except that YHWH comes, in the midst of the ruin, upon the life of Baruch. His life draws the peculiar attention of YHWH. YHWH is glad to pick up Baruch's life, take him home, celebrate him, and value him. He is a trophy of war. The news to Baruch is that your life will be a treasure; you will be found and valued by YHWH. The oracle speaks only in a metaphor; it does not spell out any specificity of that promise. Perhaps this hope is still inchoate. Perhaps the oracle says no more than that YHWH would not abandon the faithful. The faithful Baruch is an exception to the general disorder. He is a *trophy* amid the catas-*trophe*!

We may notice that the phrase "your life as a prize of war" is used by Jeremiah only one other time. Jeremiah speaks the same words to Ebed-melech, the Ethiopian who in 38:7–13 had rescued Jeremiah from death in a cistern, where he had been detained and where he "sank in the mud" (38:6). In the oracle of 39:16–18 there is again a great devastation to come, and yet again there is an adversative conjunctive "but" that interrupts the devastation with a declaration of assurance to the Ethiopian who had saved him.

Thus Baruch and Ebed-melech are singled out for an alternative future apart from the general destruction that is sure to come.

Nothing specific is offered. Jeremiah clearly cannot believe that in the end zealous fidelity does not yield good outcomes. He cannot believe that devastation is the end of the story, because there is always YHWH's prospect of "plant and build." At least in these particular texts, Baruch and Ebed-melech are the carriers of that historical possibility for this God of whom the prophet could affirm, "Nothing is too hard for you" (32:17).

Thus we may conclude that Baruch and Ebed-melech become for Jeremiah representative figures of an ongoing community of the faithful. They will not arrive at "great things," but they will be valued and treasured in the governance of YHWH. The two of them are, in vague way, carriers of Jeremiah's bid of faith in the future. The word for such a historical presence is *remnant*, those who have escaped and lived to tell of it. Neither Ebed-melech nor Baruch here ever gives voice to his faith. Ebed-melech never speaks, and Baruch speaks only as he is quoted in the lament of 45:3. They are simply those who have "hung in there" and refused to accommodate the self-destructive ideology of the dominant opinion. They surely will be the seed of a faithful future. We may imagine that this *minority of fidelity* shows up repeatedly in the story of God's people. It surely shows up in the quarrelsome restoration of Ezra and Nehemiah. Eventually it yields the roster of hopers in Hebrews 11, those who "walked by faith" in spite of every negative circumstance. The outcome, in every instance of such risk, is that judgment and despair cannot be the last word. Perhaps that claim has already been anticipated in the throwaway line of Jeremiah 4:27, with its disjunctive conjunction: "The whole land [whole earth?] shall be a desolation; *yet* I will not make a full end." The "yet" of hope has the last word! It is the minority of fidelity that precludes the "full end" of YHWH's exasperation with YHWH's people.

Questions for Discussion

1. Is fidelity always a minority report?

2. Can you identify modern-day examples of Baruch and Ebed-melech?

3. What do you make of Baruch's "reward"?

Chapter 24

Fallen, Fallen Is Babylon
(Jeremiah 50:2)

Declare among the nations and proclaim,
set up a banner and proclaim,
do not conceal it, say:
Babylon is taken,
Bel is put to shame,
Merodach is dismayed.
Her images are put to shame,
her idols are dismayed.

> ### *Scripture Passages for Reference*
>
> Jeremiah 50:35–38
> Jeremiah 51:15–23
> Isaiah 40:9
> Isaiah 52:7
> Amos 1–2
> Psalm 96:10
> Revelation 18

At the outset, Jeremiah is appointed "over nations and over kingdoms" (1:10). His attention to nations and kingdoms is most explicit in the collection of Oracles against the Nations in Jeremiah 46–51. In the end, Jeremiah asserts the lordship of YHWH over both nations and over Israel. (This is a recurring theme in the prophets; see Amos

1–2, Isaiah 13–23, and Ezekiel 25–32; see the same accent in liturgical expression in Psalm 96:10.) The corpus of Oracles against the Nations is by design focused on the two superpowers of the time: at the outset Egypt (46), superpower to the south, and at the conclusion Babylon (50–51), superpower to the north. Between Egypt (46) and Babylon (50–51) is a series of oracles concerning lesser states (47–49). In every case the prophet declares that the named state is answerable to the rule of YHWH, and in every case there is specificity concerning the defeat and demise of the named state. The rhetoric of such victory for YHWH and defeat for the state is the expansive celebrative language of military victory; the essential counterpoint that is sometimes stated and sometimes implied is awareness that the defeat of the state amounts to good news and emancipation for Israel.

As we have seen, the book of Jeremiah is preoccupied with the rise and power of Babylon and its ruler, Nebuchadnezzar. Early on there is allusion to Babylon (1:13; 5:15–17; 6:22–23). From 21:1–2 forward there is direct reference to Babylon as a rising power and consequently as a rising threat to Judah, given Babylon's expansive foreign-military policy. That much is clear geopolitically. The distinctive accent of Jeremiah, however, is not simply on geopolitics, though he is not innocent of or indifferent to such matters. Beyond that observable reality, however, Jeremiah's primary accent is the daring affirmation that Babylon will act as an instrument of YHWH's will, for it is YHWH's intent to punish Israel-Judah for its foolish and arrogant policies that contradict the will of YHWH. Thus *Babylon's geopolitical ambition* coheres, in the purview of Jeremiah, with *the intent of YHWH*; one cannot separate these two accents in Jeremiah's rhetoric. Jeremiah, moreover, believes that resistance against mighty Babylon is foolish; the wise (as well as obedient) response to Babylon is submission. The royal leadership of Jerusalem, however, refuses to submit, and brings upon itself the brutal assault of Babylon. We may entertain the possibility that the brief oracle of chapter 45 was at some point the end of the book of Jeremiah. In such an ending the last word would be "disaster on all flesh" as a judgment enacted by Babylon (45:5). That suggested ending is, moreover, credible when we remember that chapters 46–51 in the Greek translation are placed in the midst of chapter 25 and not at the end of the book.

But of course as we have it, the book of Jeremiah does not end in chapter 45. We may suppose, moreover, that at some moment the book of Jeremiah ended in 51:64 with the concluding formula "Thus far the words of Jeremiah." In its present form we can see that the entire book of Jeremiah moves toward the oracle of chapters 50–51 concerning Babylon. All through the book of Jeremiah Babylon has been YHWH's tool and ally. All that time, moreover, Babylon was surely feared and hated by the people of Judah, because it was an exploitative occupying force.

But now, abruptly, the oracle of chapters 50–51 celebrates a reversal on the part of YHWH and therefore a deep historical reversal. The introduction to the extended oracle, in verse 50:2, is a celebrative report on the dramatic defeat of Babylon. This verse begins with a series of imperatives that dispatch a messenger to bring the news home: *declare, proclaim, set up, proclaim, do not conceal.* The news is urgent and welcome as it is urgent. The news to be shared is that "Babylon is taken." Babylon is defeated! This is what CNN would call "breaking news." The technology for the delivery of news was of course different then. It required the sending of a messenger to run home with the news from the battlefield. This poetic verse of news goes on to assert that the defeat of Babylon amounted to a defeat of Babylonian gods—Bel and Merodach—who could not withstand the force of YHWH's will. Thus the outcome of the human battle is matched, in poetic affirmation, by the outcome of a battle between the gods in which YHWH prevails. The prose commentary on the news in 50:3 provides a historical explanation for the abrupt victory of YHWH. The defeat of Babylon, accomplished by YHWH, was done historically speaking by a nation "out of the north"—namely, Persia, led by Cyrus.

The defeat of Babylon by Cyrus and the Persians marked a decisive turning point in the history of Israel and the ancient world more generally. Whereas Babylon (Nebuchadnezzar) is feared and hated, Cyrus is welcomed—in biblical tradition as the "messiah" (Isaiah 45:1), who permitted the deported Jews to return to their homeland (see 2 Chronicles 36:22–23). Thus we witness a complete inversion of historical reality. That inversion is more fully voiced in the poetry of Isaiah as "gospel news":

> Get you up to a high mountain,
>   O Zion, herald of *good tidings*;
> lift up your voice with strength,
>   O Jerusalem, herald of *good tidings*,

> lift it up, do not fear;
> say to the cities of Judah,
> *"Here is your God!"*
>> Isaiah 40:9

> How beautiful upon the mountains
> are the feet of the messenger who announces peace,
> who brings *good news*,
> who announces salvation,
> who says to Zion, *"Your God reigns."*
>> Isaiah 52:7

Indeed, the biblical phrasing of the term "gospel" is evoked especially to celebrate this YHWH-inspired victory of Cyrus over Babylon that will permit a homecoming for deported Jews. This is a real defeat of the real enemy by the rule of God who governs in, with, and under the historical process.

It should be noticed that in Revelation 18 there is a celebration of the defeat of Babylon long after the disappearance of Babylon. That mighty empire now serves as a metaphor:

> "Fallen, fallen is Babylon the great!
> It has become a dwelling place of demons,
> a haunt of every foul spirit,
> a haunt of every foul bird,
> a haunt of every foul and hateful beast."
> . . . .
> "Alas, alas, the great city,
> Babylon, the mighty city!"

> For in one hour your judgment has come.
>> Revelation 18:2, 10

In context, this reference to "Babylon" is an allusion to the feared, hated power of the Roman Empire. The gospel in the book of Revelation is hope that the rule of God will defeat the feared evil power of the Roman Empire.

Our oracle concerning Babylon in the book of Jeremiah does not debate what evoked YHWH's radical turn against Babylonian power. In Isaiah 47:6-7, however, the poet provides an explanation:

> I gave them into your hand,
> you showed them no mercy;

on the aged [the most vulnerable] you made your yoke
exceedingly heavy.
You said, "I shall be mistress forever,"
so that you did not lay these things to heart
or remember their end.

According to the poet, Babylon was given great freedom by
YHWH; Babylon, however, deployed its great YHWH-given power
in unrestrained ways and with great arrogance. Babylon was unwilling or unable to recognize that there are real limits to historical possibility that, in prophetic horizon, are imposed by the Lord of history.

When those limits are transgressed, big trouble comes, even to a
superpower. It is the great seduction of superpowers to overreach in
an assumption of unrestrained limitless autonomy. Without any theological reference, Paul Kennedy has traced the way in which a series
of Western superpowers—Spain, the Netherlands, Great Britain—
came to sorry ends because of overinvestment in military budgets
that were unsustainable, in an effort at foolproof national security.
Kennedy clearly means to offer a warning to U.S. exceptionalism
that imagines it can have its unfettered way in the world, propelled
by unrestrained overspending that will lead, as it did in Europe, to its
own nullification as a great power. (Kennedy wrote this before climate change was recognized as a great risk for self-indulgent superpowers.) He homes in on the absurd investment of lives and energy
in Vietnam as a fantasy of indulgent self-regard by a superpower that
imagines it has limitless resources for the imposition of its will.[1]

It is not surprising that Jeremiah's oracle against Babylon, expansive in its celebrative tone, should include powerful artistic surges.
Here are three to which attention might be paid: First, in *50:35–38*
the poet offers a rhythmic summons of military force against Babylon
with the repeated statement "a sword, a sword, a sword, a sword."
He anticipates a military mobilization that will overcome Babylon's
vaunted military might, because Babylon goes "mad over idols" (v.
38). Second, in *51:15–19* he reiterates the poetic lines of 10:12–16. In
chapter 10, the attack on idols concerned the Israelite appeal to idols.
Now the same poetry concerns the idols of Babylon and ends with
an affirmation of the special, differentiated identity of Israel in the
economy of YHWH. Third, in *51:20–23* the repeated "with you" is
an assertion that Israel is a weapon of YHWH that will defeat nations

and kingdoms. The poetry is unrestrained in its appeal to military imagery, because the working of YHWH is in the sphere of Realpolitik. There can be no escape into private or otherworldly categories.

Given this sum of powerful poetry, we should not try to parse it in a close analytical way; we should rather let the expansive, confident rhetoric wash over us in celebration of YHWH's historical emancipation. As we do so, however, we U.S. readers should be acutely aware that the stance of the poetry is not a celebration of a superpower. To the contrary, it is the exuberant voice of underlings too long subjected to the arrogant will of a superpower that now happily acknowledges that the resolved will of YHWH can withstand and overcome even the seeming absolute force of a superpower too long inured to its own way in the world. This hard word concerning the superpower yields a very good future for the vulnerable people of YHWH, who now are free and empowered. The poet is now able to affirm that the deported are on their way home:

> They shall ask the way to Zion, with faces turned toward it, and they shall come and join themselves to the LORD by an everlasting covenant that will never be forgotten. (50:5)

It is a deep prophetic conviction that YHWH is a sure ground of hope for those who have no other hope for their future. Such hope sustains the vulnerable in the face of the strong, and the poor in the face of the rich. The good news is that history is kept open for possibility even as the superpower, always again, seeks to close off history in its own arrogance against the powerless. It is no wonder that the book of Jeremiah ends in jubilation for those now freed from the greedy exploitation of the superpower!

Questions for Discussion

1. Where has "Babylon" fallen in the past?

2. What is "Babylon" today?

3. What "Babylons" need to fall in our time?

4. What do you make of God both using and then judging Babylon?

Chapter 25

The Scroll of Disaster
(Jeremiah 51:64)

"And say, 'Thus shall Babylon sink, to rise no more, because of the disasters that I am bringing on her.'"

Thus far are the words of Jeremiah.

Scripture Passages for Reference

Jeremiah 50:33–34
Jeremiah 51:58–64

There is a finality to the verdict of the Oracles against the Nations (Jeremiah 46–51). With particular reference to Babylon there is certitude that YHWH's action (albeit via Cyrus the Persian) against Babylon will entail the defeat, humiliation, and nullification of Babylonian power:

> Thus says the LORD of hosts:
> The broad wall of Babylon
>   shall be leveled to the ground,
> and her high gates
>   shall be burned with fire.
> The peoples exhaust themselves for nothing,
>   and the nations weary themselves only for fire.
>
> 51:58

In the end the great superpower will have wearied itself with posturing, but to no avail. YHWH will prevail against all that contradicts YHWH's sovereign will. The ancillary certitude of such a verdict is that Israel will be rescued:

> The people of Israel are oppressed, and so too are the people of Judah; all their captors have held them fast and refuse to let them go. Their Redeemer is strong; the LORD of hosts is his name. He will surely plead their cause, that he may give *rest* to the earth, but *unrest* to the inhabitants of Babylon. (50:33–34)

With the phrasing of "rest" and "unrest" we may notice the contrast between weary Babylon and unwearied Israel that lives by hope:

> The nations *weary* themselves only for fire.
> 51:58

> Those who wait for the LORD shall renew their strength,
>   they shall mount up with wings like eagles,
> they shall run and *not be weary*,
>   they shall walk and not faint.
> Isaiah 40:31

In light of that finality and certitude, we may be surprised that the book of Jeremiah adds beyond the oracle a narrative confirmation of the demise of Babylon (51:59–64). It is likely that the concluding formula of verse 64 constituted the end of the book of Jeremiah. This is likely given the fact that the material of Jeremiah 52 is appropriated from the historylike narrative of 2 Kings 24:1–25:21, 27–30. (The only verses not so borrowed, 52:28–30, will be considered next in our discussion.)

In this narrative confirmation, we observe the prophet authorizing a symbolic act the performance of which demonstrates and bears witness to the real-world action. Such symbolic acts are recurring for Jeremiah. He wears a loincloth (13:1–11), visits a potter's house (18:1–11), smashes a clay pot (19:1–13), exhibits two baskets of figs (24:1–3), and wears a wooden yoke (28:10). We may consider such acts as street theater with a pedagogical intent; or we may surmise, in a more poetic way, that these dramatic acts were taken to evoke and accomplish the signified action.

Either way, the work in this brief narrative is to confirm and ensure the demise of Babylon. That work is carried out by Seriah, son of Neriah (51:59). Of special interest is the fact that Seriah is the brother of Baruch, the faithful sidekick of Jeremiah. We may conclude two things from this relationship. First, the two sons of Seriah were scribes who had a capacity for writing and who produced scrolls that constituted important historical witnesses. They are the agents through which the oral work of Jeremiah became durable written testimony for the future. Second, the two sons of Neriah were part of the faithful and loyal entourage of Jeremiah that also included the family of Shaphan and his grandson Gedaliah. This company indicates that Jeremiah was a point person for a significant political opinion that steadfastly resisted the foolish policies of the crown.

What specifically matters in the narrative, however, is the *command of Jeremiah* and the *performative action of Seriah*. While Seriah does the deed, the authorization of the deed belongs to the prophet. His word consists both in the words to be uttered by the scribe and the action to be taken by the scribe. The words constitute yet another scathing prophetic anticipation of the end of the superpower that will be terminated by the will and action of YHWH. There can be no doubt about the ultimate sovereign who will eventually not tolerate a recalcitrant empire, not even one that had earlier served as a tool for that sovereign. The action to be performed by Seriah concerns a scroll weighted by a stone that will sink into the Euphrates River. There is surely intended irony in YHWH's "administration" of the Euphrates River, for that river was the lifeblood of Babylon and marked the boundary of the state. YHWH, however, is easily a transgressor of such boundaries, for all the earth is subject to the governance of YHWH.

The action is quick. We can imagine the scroll of disaster, weighted by a stone, sinking quickly into the river. There would be a long pause as the water enveloped the scroll, even as YHWH's will engulfed the empire. We can listen and hear the bubbles of water closing over the scroll. That action, perforce, is to be accomplished with the utterance of the scribe according to prophetic instruction. The operational word is "sink." The empire is inundated by the chaotic waters in a scene not unlike the engulfment of Pharaoh (Exodus 15:8–10). Superpowers are quite transient. In their wealth and power and hubris, they imagine themselves to exist in perpetuity—like the German Third Reich for a thousand years! Prophetic faith attests otherwise. Not even the most wealthy, most powerful superpower can outflank the vagaries of history that may carry the will of the creator God. The sinking of Babylon is permanent and irreversible: "Rise no more!" The Hebrew text adds, perhaps superfluously, "They wearied themselves." It is wearying indeed to manage the stubborn realities of the historical process that refuse imperial management. The old wisdom teachers had already discerned this inscrutable reality about the historical process:

> No wisdom, no understanding, no counsel,
>   can avail against the LORD.
> The horse is made ready for the day of battle,
>   but the victory belongs to the LORD.
>   Proverbs 21:30–31

Superpowers, however, keep relearning this truth belatedly, as did the United States in Vietnam, as did the Soviet Union in Afghanistan, as is the United States most recently in Afghanistan. History is not finally or fully subject to absolute human control. There is always a wild card. Israel's name for that improbable wild card is "YHWH," the one who overthrew the absolute force of Pharaoh and who eventually showed up even against Rome on Easter Day.

The editors of the book of Jeremiah concluded that nothing more could be said or needed to be said about the ultimate disposal of the superpower. Jeremiah had no more to say, because he had, as anticipated in 1:3, walked Israel into the abyss of exile. And now from the banks of the Euphrates, he has walked Israel out of that abyss—beyond the power of Babylonian governance. The plucking up and tearing down of Jerusalem has been real and beyond denial or resistance; in the end, planting and building will prevail. Jeremiah has fulfilled the twin charges of his call (1:10). It is no wonder that this ending of the book of Jeremiah caused Jeremiah's word to linger as Israel's future was reignited after Babylon (see 2 Chronicles 36:12, 22). The scroll of Jeremiah persists with authority after the stone-weighted scroll concerning Babylon has disappeared into the silt of the Euphrates.

Questions for Discussion

1. Why do you think the prophets occasionally use sign actions? Why is their additional presence necessary? What does it add?

2. How do superpowers overestimate themselves? Why do they do so?

3. Can you identify places where the "wild card" of God exists beyond the biblical examples of exodus and Easter?

Chapter 26

Total Deported: 4,600
(Jeremiah 52:30)

All the persons were four thousand six hundred.

Scripture Passages for Reference

Jeremiah 52:15, 28–30
Ezra 2:1–67

The scroll of Jeremiah likely ended with the formula of closure in 51:64. Now added to the scroll is the appendix of chapter 52, which largely consists in a historical summary of the final days of the independent monarchy of Judah. For the most part that historical material is borrowed from the final paragraphs of 2 Kings. It includes one more reiteration of the judgment of YHWH as the cause of the devastation of Jerusalem (v. 3), and what is perhaps a hint of hope (vv. 31–34). The only part of this chapter that is not echoed from 2 Kings is the one summary paragraph of verses 28–30. For this material we have no literary parallel, so these verses present what is perhaps quite distinct historical data.

Verses 28–30 report that there were three deportations from Jerusalem to Babylon. The dates of these deportations are reckoned from the beginning date of Nebuchadnezzar's rise to power in 605 BCE. This reference point indicates the extent to which Babylon had come to occupy the imagination of Israel. The first deportation (on which see 2 Kings 24:10–17) was in 598 BCE. This group of 3,023 persons constituted the "good figs" of Jeremiah 24:1–10. It is this group that carries the hope of the book of Jeremiah. The second deportation of 832 persons was in 587 BCE (on which see 2 Kings 25:1–21). This deportation constitutes the final end of the Davidic monarchy as King Zedekiah is taken away in brutal captivity. The third deportation in 582 BCE, consisting in 745 persons, is otherwise unreported in the texts of Israel. We know of it only here and so know nothing else about it—except that this further deportation likely reflects, yet again, Babylonian response to Judean resistance to Babylonian domination. The sum of 3,023 persons in 598, 832 persons in 587, and 745 persons in 582 nicely adds up to the round number of 4,600 deportees. We have no way to verify these numbers, though the even sum of them strikes one as perhaps secondarily concocted.

Three matters may be observed about this brief paragraph. First, the paragraph follows verse 27 with its formula of closure: "So Judah went into exile out of the land." In verses 28–30 we get the word "exile" three more times, as though the text wants the term pounded into our imagination. As a consequence, this fourfold usage of "exile," reinforced by a fifth use in verse 31, shows that the anticipation of 1:3 is now fully implemented: "until the captivity of Jerusalem." The entire book of Jeremiah is about the abyss of exile; this literature serves to make that abyss the defining event in the memory of Israel. That event signifies that not even "chosenness" can give Israel a pass from the requirements of the creator/covenant-making God. No depth of "exceptionalism" offers a guarantee amid the vagaries of history.

Second, we may be struck by the precision of the numbers, a precision we of course cannot verify. Perhaps the precision is a reflection of the careful records kept by the Babylonians, a harbinger of the meticulous records kept by the Nazis about the population of the death camps. Empires specialize in statistics! More likely these exact numbers reflect the fact that membership among the deportees, in subsequent generations, became a point of pride, for the deportees are said in this tradition to be the carriers of faithful Judaism. Thus of these 4,600 persons the text can declare, "So Judah went into exile" (52:27). This is Judah! These are the real Judeans. These are the real Jews!

A few generations later, having one's name or the name of someone from one's family among the deportees became a matter of both pride and precision (Ezra 2:1–67). Indeed, that list is so precise that it includes the exact number of servants, singers, horses, mules, camels, and donkeys. Everything and everyone must be counted and accounted for! While going into exile surely was an onerous fate, being remembered as among the deportees was surely a point of honor and pride. We can see further that such a list of pride and precision soon morphed into a claim of being "holy seed" not contaminated by Gentile kinfolk (Ezra 9:2). This was of course before the capacity to do scientific tracing of family genes. But the point is clear. These are the ones who kept themselves pure and uncontaminated by "mixed blood." It is easy to see why the data in Jeremiah 52 would be careful and exact, even if that "official count" may be a fabrication.

Third, we may notice how few were deported. If we did not have this data, we might imagine a great throng of deportees. This list, however, is small enough to see that it constituted the company of "the best and the brightest," the best connected and—from the point of view of the empire—the most dangerous. (Along with them it is said that the deportees included "some of the poorest of the people" [52:15].) After all, when an invading force occupies territory, it need not fear the common folk. The threat of resistance comes from the elite who are accustomed to being in control. This small roster of deportees likely includes those whom the empire had identified as the greatest threat and therefore the ones to be deported most urgently.

This small number of deportees causes us to notice that a much larger population was left in the land. Babylon did not intend and could not and did not need to deport or eliminate the population of the land. Thus it is reported that

> Nebuzaradan the captain of the guard left some of the poorest people of the land to be vinedressers and tillers of the soil. (52:16)

The ones who remained included the peasants who were accustomed to subsistence living and who constituted no threat to Babylon but could continue the ongoing agricultural economy that perhaps would yield revenue for the occupying force. Already in 39:10 we have been told that Nebuzaradan, Babylon's military leader, has left such peasants in the land:

> Nebuzaradan the captain of the guard left in the land of Judah
> some of the poor people who owned nothing, and gave them vine-
> yards and fields at the same time.

They "owned nothing"! They were not players in the economy and
therefore had no social or political clout. They were the ones who
were now given land in an act of reappropriation. We might even
imagine that these subsistence peasants welcomed the Babylonians
as deliverers from the predatory power of Judean landowners.

In any case, the stage is set for an ongoing tension between *the
elites* who were carried away and *the peasants* who remained behind
who did not make the list of those who were included in the company of pride and precision. That tension would focus on competing
claims of faithfulness. It would also keep alive the durable question
of the extent to which and the ways in which *Jewishness* is linked to
land. For those included in the list of pride and precision, the claim
of Jewishness was not about land but about pure Torah obedience.
The tilt of the book of Jeremiah is toward the small population of
"good figs"—exiles who constitute the future of Jerusalem (Jeremiah
24). George Steiner gives contemporary expression to that tension
between those in the land and those who had only the text of Torah:

> The tensions, the dialectical relations between an unhoused at-
> homeness in the text, between the dwelling-place of the script on
> the one hand (wherever in the world a Jew reads and meditates
> Torah *is* the true Israel), and the territorial mystery of the native
> land, of the promised strip of land on the other, divide Jewish
> consciousness.[1]

The text of Jeremiah exposes this tension and comes down on
the side of the exiles who live in and through the text, a social reality that makes the scroll of Jeremiah so pivotal for that population.
It is also why it was important that Jeremiah "added many similar
words" (36:32). Steiner is a true heir of Jeremiah in this regard. He
not only re-voices the tension but gives a decisive tilt toward the
text-based exiles:

> The royal city, the nation are laid waste; the text and its transmit-
> ter endure, *there* and *now.* The Temple may be destroyed; the text
> which it housed sings in the winds that scatter them.[2]

Steiner, moreover, pushes the matter toward contemporary Judaism with his cold wonderment concerning contemporary *landed* Judaism:

> The imperilled brutalized condition of the present State of Israel, the failure of Israel to be Zion, prove the spurious, the purely expedient temporality of its re-establishment in 1948. There were, then, armed men about and politicians. The Messiah was nowhere in sight. Thus the State of Israel, as it stands today, neither fulfills nor disproves the Mosaic and prophetic covenant of return. The time is not yet.[3]

It turns out that the "exile," in the purview of Jeremiah and his legacy, was *a devastating fate* as well as *an odd vocation and a durable destiny*. All of this, according to 52:30, was transmitted only by 4,600 Jews.

Questions for Discussion

1. Why was exile a devastating fate?

2. Can you make sense of "a devastating fate" that was also "an odd vocation and a durable destiny"?

3. How and where does the believing community of today privilege the text?

Chapter 27

Released from Prison
(Jeremiah 52:31)

In the thirty-seventh year of the exile of King Jehoiachin of Judah, in the twelfth month, on the twenty-fifth day of the month, King Evil-merodach of Babylon, in the year he began to reign, showed favor to King Jehoiachin of Judah and brought him out of prison.

Scripture Passages for Reference

Jeremiah 52:31–34
2 Kings 25:27–30
Isaiah 54:7–8
Matthew 1:11

The book of Jeremiah ends with Judah in exile. King Zedekiah was deported in 587 BCE, and there is nothing more to say (52:11–27). In imitation of 2 Kings 25:27–30, however, the book of Jeremiah adds an unanticipated paragraph (52:31–34).

We know that King Jehoiachin was exiled in 598, the eighth year of Nebuchadnezzar (2 Kings 24:10–17). The young king, only eighteen years old, presided over a large entourage that was deported with him. In Jeremiah 52:31, that king still presides over the community of exiles in Babylon thirty-seven years later (561). Nebuchadnezzar has died and has been replaced by Evil-merodach as king of

Babylon Now the boy king of Judah is no longer young. He is still king in exile, but he is still in exile.

The abrupt news of verse 31 is that the long-exiled king of Judah is now recognized by the new king of Babylon at the start of his reign. This new and inexplicable recognition of the exiled king is expressed in two phrases. The first is in verse 31, where the phrase "showed favor" is in Hebrew "lifted his head." The phrase here is reminiscent of its usage in Genesis 39, wherein the narrative makes use of the ambiguity of the phrase. In Genesis 39:12 and 20, the cup-bearer to Pharaoh has his "head lifted" by Pharaoh and is restored to his role. Conversely in Genesis 39:19 and 23, the chief baker has his "head lifted" from him and is hanged. Thus the phrase refers to the life-or-death power of a king to give restorative recognition to one who had been abased by royal power. Jehoiachin, a long-time exiled king, has been abased by Nebuchadnezzar. But now the new Babylonian king reverses his fortune to bring him to the royal dining room. The second phrase of rehabilitation is that the Babylonian king, Evil-merodach, "spoke kindly" to the exiled king—that is, "promised him good." Both phrases suggest restoration and rehabilitation, with affirmation of the title and role of the exiled king.

We do not know what prompted this restorative act by Evil-merodach. Apparently the mighty king of Babylon had in his company "other kings" (v. 32) who had been conquered and were also subservient to and dependent upon Babylonian favor. The matter of restoration is open-ended and ambiguous. It is possible that dining at the royal table every day might have been to keep the kings under surveillance to prevent any organized resistance to Babylonian power. Or perhaps the Babylonian king enjoyed exhibiting the many kings over whom he presided. It is also possible, however, that the narrative intends to affirm that the exiled king of Judah is recognized and so may have a possible future as a restored ruler. This third option of royal restoration (for which there is no evidence beyond this paragraph) has been famously embraced by Gerhard von Rad, who acknowledges that this text does not and cannot know the future but wants to leave open the historical possibility for a restored future for the Davidic house: "The one thing he [the narrator] could do was just, in this direction, not to close the door of history, but to leave it open."[1] One should not overstate von Rad's positive judgment because this is no assurance of restoration, only the possibility.

We know that elsewhere the book of Jeremiah has been deeply and variously engaged with the Davidic house. Jeremiah has celebrated King Josiah as a faithful agent of justice for the poor (22:15–16). He has castigated King Jehoiakim as a doer of injustice and unrighteousness (22:13–19). He has had to negotiate with King Zedekiah, whom he did not easily trust (37:17–21; 38:14–16). Most important for 52:31, he had declared that Jehoiachin (aka Coniah) in exile would have no heir:

> Is this man Coniah a despised broken pot,
>   a vessel no one wants?
> Why are he and his offspring hurled out
>   and cast away in a land they do not know?
> . . . .
> Record this man as childless,
>   a man who shall not succeed in his days;
> for none of his offspring shall succeed
>   in sitting on the throne of David,
>   and ruling again in Judah.
>   22:28–30

That hard word would seem to make any hope in 52:31 moot. That verse, moreover, does not go so far as to claim that Jehoiachin will have any heir—except that the book of Jeremiah, likely beyond the person of the prophet, does anticipate a future Davidic king who will rule justly:

> The days are surely coming, says the LORD, when I will raise up for David a righteous Branch, and he shall reign as king and deal wisely, and shall execute justice and righteousness in the land. (23:5)

> In those days and at that time I will cause a righteous Branch to spring up for David; and he shall execute justice and righteousness in the land. (33:15; see also 33:17–26)

These promises, of course, do not tell us how to get from *there* (exile) to *here* (restoration). Thus we can see that in the book of Jeremiah, kingship and a royal future are deeply contested matters, with many opinions voiced. We can observe, in any case, that the exile is not the end of the story, as Judaism did continue and thrive. The exile is a disruption—a deep disruption, an abyss!—but it is not a termination. Thus, for example, later on Isaiah will have God express both *honesty* about what has happened and future-creating *compassion*:

> For a brief moment I abandoned you,
>   but with great compassion I will gather you.
> In overflowing wrath for a moment
>   I hid my face from you,
> but with everlasting love I will have compassion on you,
>   says the LORD, your Redeemer.
>
> Isaiah 54:7–8

That promise of restoration may take many different forms; it is not at all assured that the royal house will figure in such a future. But von Rad is right that a royal prospect is also not foreclosed in these poetic anticipations.

The prospect of royal restoration, left open by Jeremiah 52:31, has served the hope of Jerusalem that "Messiah will come." Beyond the hopes of Judaism, moreover, that open-ended hope has been operative in Christian faith, as the earliest church made its claim that Jesus was the awaited Messiah. In the genealogy of Matthew, King Jehoiachin (Jechoniah) is a part of the pedigree that connects Israel's royal line to "Jesus, the Messiah, son of David, son of Abraham" (Matthew 1:1, 11). But of course the listing that makes Jesus "son of David" is problematic at best (see Matthew 1:16) and has more to do with popular acclamation of Jesus than any claim he made about himself and his identity (see Mark 10:47–48).

The most we can say of this quite unexpected "historical note" in our verse is that an opening is left for the future. That opening, moreover, does not depend on the pedigree or privileges of the royal house. It depends, rather, on the faithfulness of YHWH. What we know of the faithfulness of YHWH, moreover, is that YHWH can work in, with, and under social institutions (such as monarchy). Conversely, YHWH is not confined or captivated in any such institution, certainly not in monarchy or temple.

In his reflection on Israel's hope as it runs toward the New Testament, Gerhard von Rad notices how Israel's sweeping hope in YHWH soars:

She [Israel] thus swelled Jahweh's promises to an infinity. . . . Placing absolutely no limit on God's power yet to fulfil, she transmitted promises still unfulfilled to generations to come.[2]

And then von Rad connects this powerful hope specifically to 52:31:

Were the acts of guidance and chastisement, the saving orders which were so strong a feature of the monarchical period, finally justified by an unhappy king's being allowed at the last to put off his prison clothes and to sit as a vassal at the table of the king of Babylon (II Kings xxv 27ff.)?[3]

My impression is that in its final editing, the makers of the book of Jeremiah could not end this account in exile. They could not do so because YHWH is faithful to YHWH's promise. They could not do so, moreover, because the ongoing future of Judaism required otherwise. History, an arena of YHWH's purposes, leaves ajar a door for the future. The reader of the book of Jeremiah may look with eager longing for the appearance of "justice and righteousness," the recurring mandate of the royal house (23:5–6; 33:15). One might conclude that wherever justice and righteousness are evident in the political economy of the world, there the future-creating work of God is operative. Every editor of the book and every reader of the book must hasten to catch up with the future-creating God who will not let history end in exile—in the abyss—but who, instead, *returns*.

Questions for Discussion

1. Where is there evidence that God has left the door open?

2. Where do you see God being faithful to the promises of old?

3. Where do you see traces of "exile" ending?

4. Why will God not let history end in exile and abyss?

Notes

SERIES FOREWORD

1. See, among other publications, Walter Brueggemann, *A Commentary on Jeremiah: Exile and Homecoming* (Grand Rapids, MI: Eerdmans, 1998); *Like Fire in the Bones: Listening for the Prophetic Word in Jeremiah*, ed. Patrick D. Miller (Minneapolis: Fortress, 2006); *The Theology of the Book of Jeremiah*, Old Testament Theology (New York: Cambridge University Press, 2007); *Preaching Jeremiah: Announcing God's Restorative Passion* (Minneapolis: Fortress, 2020); and the present volume.

2. On what follows, see further chapter 16 in the present volume.

3. See Ellen F. Davis, "Exploding the Limits: Form and Function in Psalm 22," *Journal for the Study of the Old Testament* 17 (1992): 93–105.

4. Marilyn Chandler McEntyre, *What's in a Phrase? Pausing Where Scripture Gives You Pause* (Grand Rapids, MI: Eerdmans, 2014).

5. McEntyre, x.

6. McEntyre, x.

7. McEntyre, x.

8. The word occurs no less than forty-one times in Mark: 1:10, 12, 18, 20, 21, 23, 28, 29, 30, 42, 43; 2:8, 12; 3:6; 4:5, 15, 16, 17, 29; 5:2, 29, 30, 42 (two times); 6:25, 27, 45, 50, 54; 7:25; 8:10; 9:15, 20, 24; 10:52; 11:2, 3; 14:43, 45, 72; 15:1.

PREFACE

1. See Walter Brueggemann, *A Commentary on Jeremiah: Exile and Homecoming* (Grand Rapids, MI: Eerdmans, 1998).

CHAPTER 1: THE WORD OF THE LORD "CAME" (AND STILL DOES)

1. These familiar lines from Tennyson are from "In Memoriam of A. H. H. Obit MDCCCXXXIII (Prelude)."

CHAPTER 2: TO PLUCK UP . . . AND TO PLANT

1. "Before the Lord's Eternal Throne," *The Hymnal 1982* (New York: Church Publishing Corporation, 1985), 391. The text here is modified from the Episcopal hymnal, where it appears in a bowdlerized form.

CHAPTER 10: THE WORDS OF THIS COVENANT

1. Robert N. Bellah, *The Broken Covenant: American Civil Religion in Time of Trial* (New York: Seabury Press, 1975).

CHAPTER 12: ON KNOWING GOD

1. Peter Baker and Maggie Haberman, "Trump Belittles His Black Critics and Seeks Shield," *New York Times,* July 30, 2019, p. 1.

CHAPTER 13: FRIENDS IN HIGH PLACES

1. Robert R. Wilson, *Prophecy and Society in Ancient Israel* (Philadelphia: Fortress Press, 1980).

2. Harold Bloom, *The Anxiety of Influence: A Theory of Poetry* (Oxford: Oxford University Press, 1973).

CHAPTER 14: BEHIND TREASON . . . GOD?

1. "This Is My Father's World," *Glory to God: The Presbyterian Hymnal* (Louisville, KY: Presbyterian Publishing Corporation, 2013), 370.

CHAPTER 18: THE RESTORATION OF LOST LAND

1. Patrick Phillips, *Blood at the Root: A Racial Cleansing in America* (New York: Norton, 2016).

2. Vann D. Newkirk II, "The Great Land Robbery," *Atlantic*, September 2019, https://www.theatlantic.com/magazine/archive/2019/09/this-land-was-our-land/594742/.

3. Katie Rogers and Zolan Kanno-Youngs, "Trump Tells Aides 'Take the Land' as Impatience Grows on Border Wall," *New York Times*, August 28, 2019, A17.

CHAPTER 19: A RIGHTEOUS BRANCH

1. "Mine Eyes Have Seen the Glory," *Glory to God: The Presbyterian Hymnal* (Louisville, KY: Presbyterian Publishing Corporation, 2013), 354.

CHAPTER 20: MANY SIMILAR WORDS

1. George Steiner, "Our Homeland, the Text," *Salmagundi* 66 (Winter/Spring 1985): 5.

CHAPTER 24: FALLEN, FALLEN IS BABYLON

1. Paul Kennedy, *The Rise and Fall of the Great Powers: Economic Change and Military Conflict from 1500 to 2000* (New York: Random House, 1987).

CHAPTER 26: TOTAL DEPORTED: 4,600

1. George Steiner, "Our Homeland, the Text," *Salmagundi* 66 (Winter/Spring 1985): 5.
2. Steiner, 21.
3. Steiner, 23.

CHAPTER 27: RELEASED FROM PRISON

1. Gerhard von Rad, *Old Testament Theology I: The Theology of Israel's Historical Traditions* (New York: Harper & Brothers, 1962), 343n22.
2. Gerhard von Rad, *Old Testament Theology II: The Theology of Israel's Prophetic Traditions* (Edinburgh: Oliver & Boyd, 1965), 320.
3. von Rad, 320.

ϽSIA information can be obtained
ᴠww.ICGtesting.com
ιted in the USA
ɪW041944130322
Ͻ63LV00001B/1